CHL

TRAVEL GUIDE

TONYA F. MARTINS

TABLE OF CONTENTS

INTRODUCTION

GETTING TO CHIANG MAI

GETTING AROUND CHIANG MAI

ACCOMMODATION

Best Areas To Stay
- Old City
- Nimmanhaemin
- Riverside
- Santitham

Hotels
Hostels
Guesthouses

TOP ATTRACTIONS AND MUST-SEE SIGHTS

Doi Suthep
Wat Phra Singh and Wat Chedi Luang
Chiang Mai Old City and Its Ancient Walls
Chiang Mai Night Safari
Bo Sang Handicraft Village

CULTURAL EXPERIENCES AND FESTIVALS

Loy Krathong and Yi Peng Lantern Festival
Songkran
Traditional Thai Dance and Muay Thai Shows
Learning Thai Cooking at Local Schools

EXPLORING NATURE AND OUTDOOR ACTIVITIES

Doi Inthanon National Park
Elephant Sanctuaries
Zip-lining and Jungle Adventures
Trekking and Waterfall Hikes
The Mae Ping River Cruise Experience

CULINARY DELIGHTS OF CHIANG MAI

Must-Try Dishes
Street Food Markets and Where to Find Them
Best Restaurants and Hidden Eateries
Cooking Classes and Local Food Tours
Vegetarian and Vegan Dining Options

SHOPPING AND MARKETS

Night Bazaars and Artisan Markets
Warorot Market (Kad Luang) Guide
Craft Villages
Tips for Bargaining Like a Local
Buying Authentic Thai Souvenirs

CONCLUSION

Useful Phrases
Useful Apps and Websites

INTRODUCTION

Overview

Nestled in the mountainous region of northern Thailand, Chiang Mai is a vibrant city that beautifully blends ancient traditions with modern attractions. Known as the "Rose of the North," this cultural capital is beloved for its historic charm, breathtaking landscapes, and a thriving arts and culinary scene.

Once the capital of the ancient Lanna Kingdom, Chiang Mai provides visitors a journey through time, evident in its well-preserved temples, age-old city walls, and fascinating festivals. Yet, the city is also a hub of contemporary activity, with bustling markets, trendy neighborhoods, and a growing expat community.

Chiang Mai's allure is further enhanced by its natural wonders. The surrounding hills and national parks are teeming with waterfalls, hiking trails, and abundant wildlife, making it a paradise for outdoor enthusiasts and eco-travelers. Visitors can explore everything from serene elephant sanctuaries to adrenaline-pumping jungle adventures.

Weather and Climate

Chiang Mai experiences a tropical climate, characterized by three distinct seasons: the cool season, the hot season, and the rainy season. Understanding the weather patterns can help you plan your visit to make the most of your time in this beautiful city.

1. Cool Season (November to February)

Overview: The cool season is the most popular time to visit Chiang Mai, thanks to its pleasant weather. Daytime temperatures range from 20°C to 30°C (68°F to 86°F), while evenings can get as chilly as 10°C (50°F) in the higher altitudes.

What to Expect: Clear skies, low humidity, and lush greenery. This is the best time for outdoor activities, including trekking, exploring temples, and visiting the countryside. It's also festival season, with the Loy Krathong and Yi

Peng festivals drawing visitors from all over the world.

Travel Tip: Pack a light jacket or sweater for the cooler evenings, especially if you plan to visit higher elevations like Doi Suthep or Doi Inthanon.

2. Hot Season (March to June)

Overview: The hot season sees temperatures soar, with daytime highs ranging from 30°C to 40°C (86°F to 104°F). The air can become dry and hazy, especially in March and April, due to agricultural burning in the region.

What to Expect: The city can feel uncomfortably warm, making midday outdoor activities challenging. However, it's still a good time to explore waterfalls, visit mountain retreats, or take a refreshing dip in natural pools. The Thai New Year festival, Songkran, occurs in April and features a nationwide water fight, helping you cool off.

Travel Tip: Stay hydrated, use plenty of sunscreen, and wear lightweight, breathable clothing. Consider planning your activities in the early morning or late afternoon to avoid the peak heat.

3. Rainy Season (July to October)

Overview: The rainy season brings heavy, yet often short-lived, downpours. Temperatures range from 25°C to 34°C (77°F to 93°F), and the city's surroundings become a lush, vibrant green.

What to Expect: Rain showers are typically in the afternoon or evening, leaving mornings relatively clear. The countryside and waterfalls are at their most stunning, and it's a quieter time for tourism, which means fewer crowds and more affordable accommodations. However, some trekking trails may become muddy and slippery.

Travel Tip: Bring an umbrella or a light rain jacket and waterproof footwear. Be flexible with your plans in case of sudden weather changes, and check road conditions if you're heading into the mountains.

Why Visit Chiang Mai

Chiang Mai stands out as one of Thailand's most captivating destinations, extending a unique blend of cultural heritage, natural beauty, and modern vibrancy. Here's why a visit to this northern gem should be on your travel list:

1. Rich Cultural Heritage

Chiang Mai was once the capital of the Lanna Kingdom, and this history is preserved in its stunning temples, traditional architecture, and ancient city walls. The Old City is a living museum, home to over 300 Buddhist temples, including the iconic Wat Phra Singh and Wat Chedi Luang. Cultural festivals like Yi Peng and Songkran are unforgettable experiences that immerse visitors in Thai traditions.

2. Breathtaking Natural Scenery

Surrounded by lush mountains and fertile valleys, Chiang Mai is a paradise for nature lovers. Doi Suthep, with its panoramic views and sacred temple, and Doi Inthanon National Park, known as the "Roof of Thailand," are just a few of the scenic spots to explore. From serene rice paddies to rushing waterfalls and mist-shrouded peaks, the landscape here provides endless opportunities for adventure.

3. Unique Experiences with Wildlife

Chiang Mai is famous for ethical elephant sanctuaries where you can observe and care for these gentle giants in a responsible way. Visit sanctuaries that prioritize the well-being of the elephants, and take part in activities like feeding and bathing them. In addition, the region's national parks are teeming with diverse wildlife and birdwatching opportunities.

4. World-Class Cuisine

Food enthusiasts will be in heaven in Chiang Mai. The city is renowned for its vibrant street food culture and Northern Thai cuisine, featuring specialties like Khao Soi (a flavorful coconut curry noodle soup) and Sai Oua (spicy sausage). Cooking classes are widely available, extending visitors the chance to learn the art of traditional Thai cooking from local experts. Don't forget to explore the bustling night markets for a feast of flavors.

5. Affordable and Welcoming

Chiang Mai is known for being one of the most affordable travel destinations in Thailand, making it perfect for budget and luxury travelers alike. The warm hospitality of the locals adds to the city's charm, with a friendly and relaxed atmosphere that makes visitors feel at home.

6. Adventure and Outdoor Activities

Whether you're an adrenaline junkie or a casual adventurer, Chiang Mai has something for everyone. Experience thrilling zip-lining tours through the jungle canopy, trek through dense forests to reach hidden waterfalls, or enjoy a leisurely bike ride through the countryside. The cooler months also make it ideal for exploring the great outdoors.

7. Spiritual and Wellness Retreats

Chiang Mai is a haven for those seeking inner peace and wellness. Meditation centers and yoga retreats abound, providing opportunities to connect with your mind and body in tranquil settings. Many visitors also indulge in traditional Thai massages or visit herbal saunas for a truly relaxing experience.

8. Creative and Artistic Vibes

The city has a thriving arts and crafts scene, with artisan markets showcasing handmade silver jewelry, intricate wood carvings, and traditional Thai pottery. Visit creative hubs like the Nimmanhaemin area, where art galleries, boutique cafes, and trendy shops give a modern twist to the city's artistic spirit.

9. Vibrant Markets and Nightlife

Chiang Mai's markets are a sensory delight, from the famous Sunday Walking Street Market to the colorful Warorot Market. In the evening, the city comes alive with a lively nightlife scene, extending everything from laid-back riverside bars to bustling night bazaars and cultural performances.

10. Gateway to Northern Thailand

Chiang Mai is the perfect base for exploring the wider region of Northern Thailand. From here, you can take scenic day trips to nearby towns like Chiang Rai, known for its breathtaking

White Temple, or Pai, a laid-back mountain village with hot springs and incredible views. The surrounding countryside is rich in adventure and cultural experiences, making Chiang Mai a gateway to discovering the best of the North.

Best Time to Visit

Chiang Mai's tropical climate features three main seasons—cool, hot, and rainy—each extending a different experience. Knowing what to expect in each season will help you choose the perfect time for your visit.

1. Cool Season (November to February)

Overview: This is the peak tourist season, with daytime temperatures ranging from 20°C to 30°C (68°F to 86°F) and pleasantly cool nights. The weather is ideal for sightseeing, outdoor activities, and exploring Chiang Mai's cultural landmarks.

Why Visit: The cool season is perfect for trekking in the surrounding mountains, exploring bustling markets, or visiting the city's many temples. It's also when Chiang Mai hosts some of its most spectacular festivals, like the Loy Krathong and Yi Peng Lantern Festivals, which illuminate the city with thousands of floating lanterns.

Travel Tip: Make your accommodation bookings well in advance, as this is the busiest time of year. Also, pack a light jacket for the cooler mornings and evenings.

2. Hot Season (March to June)

Overview: Temperatures during the hot season can soar to 35°C to 40°C (95°F to 104°F), especially in April. The heat can be intense, but it's a great time to escape to the mountains or enjoy water-based activities.

Why Visit: The Thai New Year, Songkran, falls in mid-April and is celebrated with a massive, city-wide water fight. It's a fun and memorable experience that helps to beat the heat. Despite the high temperatures, there are plenty of shaded and indoor attractions to enjoy.

Travel Tip: Stay hydrated and avoid outdoor activities during peak midday hours. Make use of Chiang Mai's many cafes and indoor attractions to cool off.

3. Rainy Season (July to October)

Overview: The rainy season is characterized by frequent but typically short-lived downpours. Temperatures range from 25°C to 34°C (77°F to 93°F), and the landscape comes alive with lush greenery.

Why Visit: The countryside is at its most beautiful, with vibrant rice fields and cascading waterfalls. The rain also brings fewer crowds and better deals on accommodations. For nature lovers, this is a fantastic time for exploring the region's national parks and enjoying the serene atmosphere.

Travel Tip: Be prepared for sudden rain showers by carrying an umbrella or rain jacket. Some outdoor activities may be affected by the weather, so have flexible plans. The roads in the mountains can become slippery, so exercise caution if you're driving or trekking.

Cultural Overview

Chiang Mai, the cultural capital of northern Thailand, boasts a rich and diverse heritage deeply rooted in the traditions of the ancient Lanna Kingdom. The city's unique culture is reflected in its architecture, cuisine, spiritual practices, and daily life, extending visitors an authentic glimpse into the heart of northern Thai life.

1. The Lanna Heritage

Chiang Mai was founded in 1296 as the capital of the Lanna Kingdom, and its cultural influences are still prevalent today. The city is known for its distinct Lanna-style temples, characterized by intricate wood carvings, steeply pitched roofs, and elaborate murals. Key examples include Wat Phra Singh and Wat Chedi Luang, which embody the architectural beauty of this period.

2. Buddhism and Spiritual Practices

Buddhism is at the core of daily life in Chiang Mai. Monks dressed in saffron robes are a common sight, and locals practice their faith with devotion, participating in merit-making rituals and temple visits. Visitors can experience this spiritual atmosphere by visiting temples, observing meditation practices, or even joining a silent meditation retreat. Wat Phra That Doi Suthep, perched on a mountain overlooking the city, is one of the most revered pilgrimage sites.

3. Festivals and Celebrations

Chiang Mai's calendar is filled with vibrant festivals that showcase the city's rich cultural traditions. The Yi Peng Lantern Festival and Loy Krathong are two of the most magical events, where the skies and rivers are lit up with thousands of floating lanterns and decorated krathongs (floating baskets). Songkran, the Thai New Year, is another major celebration, marked by joyful water fights in the streets and traditional ceremonies at temples.

4. Traditional Arts and Crafts

Chiang Mai is a hub for traditional Lanna arts and crafts. Local artisans are skilled in creating silverware, wood carvings, pottery, and intricate textiles. The Bo Sang Handicraft Village is famous for its beautifully crafted paper umbrellas, while other nearby villages specialize in producing unique handcrafted goods. Exploring the local markets and workshops gives visitors the chance to witness these art forms and bring home one-of-a-kind souvenirs.

5. Cuisine and Food Culture

The cuisine of Chiang Mai is a highlight of the city's cultural experience. Traditional dishes like Khao Soi (a coconut curry noodle soup), Sai Oua (northern Thai sausage), and Nam Prik Ong (a spicy tomato dip) reflect the flavors and ingredients unique to the region. Food plays a significant role in social gatherings and religious extending s, with bustling night markets extending a taste of the city's culinary heritage. Participating in a cooking class is a popular way for visitors to learn about local flavors and techniques.

6. Hill Tribes and Ethnic Diversity

The mountains surrounding Chiang Mai are home to various hill tribes, each with its own unique customs, languages, and traditional dress. Tribes such as the Karen, Hmong, Akha, and Lisu have preserved their distinct ways of life, extending cultural insights through village visits and community-based tourism projects. Travelers interested in ethical and responsible tourism can engage with these communities to learn about their culture, crafts, and sustainable practices.

7. Traditional Music and Dance

Music and dance are integral to the cultural fabric of Chiang Mai. Traditional Lanna music features instruments like the khim (hammered dulcimer) and salu (a bowed string instrument), often performed during cultural ceremonies and festivals. Lanna-style dance, known for its graceful hand movements and elegant costumes, can be enjoyed at cultural centers and during special events.

8. Local Customs and Etiquette

Understanding and respecting local customs is crucial when visiting Chiang Mai. The Thai concept of "sanuk" (fun and lightheartedness) influences social interactions, while the idea of "mai pen rai" (it's okay, or don't worry) reflects a laid-back approach to life. Visitors should dress modestly when visiting temples, remove shoes before entering sacred places, and be mindful of their behavior to show respect for local traditions.

GETTING TO CHIANG MAI

By Air

International Flights

Chiang Mai International Airport welcomes direct international flights from several major Asian cities, including Bangkok, Singapore, Kuala Lumpur, Hong Kong, Seoul, Taipei, and more. Popular airlines that operate direct flights to Chiang Mai include Thai Airways, AirAsia, Scoot, and Cathay Pacific.

Price Range: Depending on your departure city, a one-way international ticket to Chiang Mai can range from:

Within Southeast Asia: $50 to $150 USD for budget airlines; $150 to $300 USD for full-service airlines.

From East Asia: $150 to $400 USD for budget and standard airlines.

From Europe or North America: Typically, there are no direct flights, so prices vary significantly. Expect to pay between $500 and $1,000+ USD for a one-way ticket with layovers in major hubs like Bangkok, Doha, or Dubai.

Domestic Flights from Bangkok

The most common way to reach Chiang Mai from within Thailand is by flying from Bangkok. Domestic flights operate frequently between Bangkok's Suvarnabhumi Airport (BKK) and Don Mueang Airport (DMK) to Chiang Mai, with flight times of approximately 1 hour and 15 minutes.

Airlines: Options include Thai Airways, Bangkok Airways, AirAsia, Nok Air, and Thai VietJet Air.

Price Range: Domestic one-way flights between Bangkok and Chiang Mai are quite affordable, typically ranging from $20 to $80 USD. Booking in advance or flying with budget airlines often results in lower prices.

Flights from Other Thai Cities

Chiang Mai is also well connected to other popular Thai destinations such as Phuket, Krabi, and Koh Samui. These flights are generally direct and take between 1.5 to 2 hours.

Phuket to Chiang Mai: $40 to $120 USD one-way.
Krabi to Chiang Mai: $30 to $100 USD one-way.
Koh Samui to Chiang Mai: $100 to $200 USD one-way (flights from Koh Samui are generally more expensive due to limited airline options).

Airport Transfers

Once you arrive at Chiang Mai International Airport, you'll find various transportation options to reach the city center, which is just a 10 to 15-minute drive away.

Airport Taxi: Approximately 150 to 200 THB ($4 to $6 USD).
Rideshare (Grab): 100 to 250 THB ($3 to $8 USD), depending on distance and time of day.
Songthaew (Red Trucks): A shared local taxi option costing around 30 to 50 THB ($1 to $1.50 USD) per person for rides into the city.

Booking Tips

Advance Booking: For international flights, booking a few months in advance can help you get better deals. Domestic flights within Thailand are generally affordable, even if booked closer to the departure date, but booking early can still save you money.
Budget Airlines: While budget carriers put forward great prices, be sure to check for extra fees on luggage, seat selection, and other add-ons.

By Train

Train Routes and Duration

Trains from Bangkok to Chiang Mai depart from Hua Lamphong Railway Station and arrive at Chiang Mai Railway Station. The journey takes between 11 to 15 hours, depending on the type of train and service class you choose.

Types of Trains

The State Railway of Thailand operates several types of trains on this route:
Special Express Trains: The fastest and most comfortable option, often preferred for overnight travel.
Express Trains: A good balance between speed and affordability.
Rapid Trains: Slower and more budget-friendly, but with fewer amenities.

Classes of Service

1. First Class:

provides private cabins with air conditioning, suitable for one or two passengers. First-class cabins have comfortable sleeping berths, personal storage, and sometimes even washbasins.
Price Range: 1,200 to 1,700 THB ($35 to $50 USD) per person.

2. Second Class:

Available in both air-conditioned and non-air-conditioned options. The sleeper cars have comfortable bunks and curtains for privacy. Seats in second-class carriages are generally more spacious and well-suited for the long journey.

Air-Conditioned Sleeper: 800 to 1,200 THB ($23 to $35 USD) per person.
Non-Air-Conditioned Sleeper: 600 to 900 THB ($18 to $27 USD) per person.
Seated Second Class: 500 to 700 THB ($15 to $20 USD) for seats instead of beds.

Third Class:

The most budget-friendly option, with basic seating and no air conditioning. The seats are often hard and can get uncomfortable for the long journey, but it's a great choice for travelers on a tight budget or for those seeking an authentic local experience.
Price Range: 200 to 400 THB ($6 to $12 USD) per person.

Overnight Train Experience

Taking an overnight sleeper train is a popular and practical choice. It saves a night's accommodation cost and allows you to arrive in Chiang Mai early in the morning, ready to explore. The sleeper berths are generally clean and come with sheets, blankets, and pillows.

The train has a dining car, and vendors occasionally board at stops to sell snacks and meals.

Booking Tips

Advance Booking: It's advisable to book your train tickets in advance, especially for first-class and second-class sleeper cars, as they are in high demand. You can book through the official State Railway of Thailand website, at Hua Lamphong Station, or through travel agencies.

Scenic Views: If you're traveling during the day, you'll be rewarded with picturesque views of the countryside, rice fields, and mountain ranges, making it a memorable experience.

By Bus

Types of Buses and Classes

Several bus companies operate routes from Bangkok to Chiang Mai, with departures from two main terminals in Bangkok: Mo Chit Bus Terminal and Southern Bus Terminal. The buses are categorized into different classes, each extending varying levels of comfort and amenities.

1. VIP Buses:

The most comfortable option, with spacious reclining seats, air conditioning, and onboard amenities like snacks, drinks, and personal entertainment systems.
Price Range: 700 to 1,000 THB ($20 to $30 USD) per person.
Features: Fewer seats per bus (usually 24 to 32), more legroom, blankets, and sometimes a meal stop included.

2. First-Class Buses:

Another comfortable option with air conditioning, reclining seats, and usually a meal stop.
Price Range: 500 to 800 THB ($15 to $23 USD) per person.

Features: Slightly more seats than VIP buses, but still comfortable for the long journey. Restroom facilities are often available onboard.

3. Second-Class Buses:

A budget-friendly option, but less spacious and usually with more stops along the way. These buses are still equipped with air conditioning, but amenities are more limited.
Price Range: 300 to 500 THB ($9 to $15 USD) per person.
Features: Standard seats, less legroom, and often no onboard restrooms.

Bus Companies

1. Nakhonchai Air: Known for their reliable service and comfortable VIP buses. They provide snacks, water, and onboard entertainment.

2. Greenbus: Another reputable company that provides first-class and second-class services to Chiang Mai.

3. Bangkok Busline: provides VIP and first-class options with comfortable seating and good customer service.

Travel Tips

Advance Booking: It is recommended to book your bus tickets in advance, especially during peak travel seasons (November to February) and around major festivals like Songkran and Loy Krathong.
Overnight Buses: Many travelers prefer taking overnight buses to save on accommodation and to arrive in Chiang Mai early in the morning. Blankets are usually provided, but it's a good idea to bring a travel pillow for added comfort.
Rest Stops: Long-distance buses typically make one or two rest stops where passengers can use restrooms and purchase food and drinks.

Booking Options

Online Booking: Tickets can be booked online through platforms like 12Go Asia or directly on the websites of bus operators.

At the Terminal: Tickets can also be purchased at Mo Chit Bus Terminal in Bangkok, but it's best to arrive early if you plan to buy tickets on the day of departure.

By Car

Driving Routes

There are two main routes to drive from Bangkok to Chiang Mai:

Route 1 (Highway 1): This is the most direct route and follows the Phahonyothin Highway (AH2), passing through cities like Nakhon Sawan and Kamphaeng Phet. It's a straightforward highway drive, but can be busy during peak hours.

Route 2 (Highway 32): A slightly longer route that takes you through rural towns and provides more scenic views. This route might take longer but provides a more relaxed drive.

Car Rental

If you don't have your own vehicle, renting a car is an easy option. Several car rental agencies operate in Bangkok and Chiang Mai, extending various types of vehicles for short- or long-term rentals.

Car Rental Agencies: Major companies like Hertz, Avis, Budget, and Thai-based companies like Sixt and Thai Rent A Car extend rental services. You can also book through international online platforms like Rentalcars and Europcar.

Price Range: The cost of renting a car in Thailand typically depends on the car type, rental duration, and season. For a basic economy car, expect to pay around:

Daily Rate: 800 to 1,500 THB ($25 to $45 USD) per day.

Weekly Rate: 4,500 to 7,000 THB ($130 to $200 USD) per week.

Additional Fees: Most rental companies include basic insurance, but additional coverage (collision damage waiver, etc.) will increase the price by 150 to 500 THB ($5 to $15 USD) per day.

Fuel Costs

Fuel prices in Thailand are generally affordable. As of recent data, the price of gasoline is around 35 to 45 THB per liter ($1 to $1.30 USD per liter). For a trip from Bangkok to Chiang Mai, you can expect to spend about 1,500 to 2,000 THB ($45 to $60 USD) on fuel, depending on the vehicle's fuel efficiency and the route taken.

Tolls and Road Conditions

Tolls: There are several toll booths along the highway between Bangkok and Chiang Mai, with a total cost of around 200 to 400 THB ($6 to $12 USD) for the entire trip, depending on your route.
Road Conditions: The highways are generally in good condition, with well-marked lanes, rest areas, and gas stations along the way. However, during the rainy season (June to October), some sections may experience flooding or slower traffic, so it's important to check road conditions before your trip.

Travel Tips for Driving to Chiang Mai

Navigation: Use a reliable GPS or a navigation app like Google Maps to guide you through the route. It's advisable to check traffic conditions before setting off, as Bangkok can have heavy traffic, especially during rush hours.
Rest Stops: Make use of the rest areas along the way to stretch, take breaks, and grab snacks.

These stops are usually equipped with food vendors and clean restrooms.

Driving Hours: It's recommended to start your drive early in the morning to avoid heavy traffic out of Bangkok and to reach Chiang Mai before dark. However, if you're planning an overnight drive, be cautious as the roads can be winding in some areas.

Alternative: Private Car with Driver

For those who prefer not to drive themselves, you can hire a private car with a driver. This option is more expensive but provides a more relaxed experience without the stress of navigating unfamiliar roads. Prices for private transfers vary depending on the service provider and the vehicle type.

Price Range: A private car transfer from Bangkok to Chiang Mai can range from 4,000 to 10,000 THB ($120 to $300 USD) one-way, depending on the car class (economy, sedan, or luxury SUV).

GETTING AROUND CHIANG MAI

Local Transportation Options

Tuk Tuks

What Are Tuk Tuks?

Tuk tuks in Chiang Mai are small, open-air vehicles with a driver and seating for up to 3 passengers (sometimes 4, depending on the size of the tuk tuk). They are a popular and convenient way to get around, especially for short trips in the city, and provide an opportunity to experience local transportation in a unique and engaging way.

Where to Find Tuk Tuks

Popular Areas: You'll find tuk tuks readily available near popular areas like the Old City, Nimmanhaemin Road, Tha Phae Gate, and the Night Bazaar.
Hotels and Tourist Attractions: Many hotels and tourist sites provide tuk tuk services, or you can simply flag one down as you walk around.

Tourist Packages: Some tuk tuk drivers provide fixed-rate tours of the city's attractions, which can be a good way to see multiple sites in a short amount of time.

Price Range

The cost of a tuk tuk ride in Chiang Mai depends on the distance, time of day, and the driver's negotiation skills. Here is a general breakdown of the price ranges:

Short Trips (1-2 kilometers): 30 to 60 THB ($1 to $2 USD) for a ride around local areas, such as from one street to another within a neighborhood or short trips to tourist attractions.
Medium Trips (3-5 kilometers): 60 to 150 THB ($2 to $4 USD) for trips that are a little longer, like traveling from the Old City to Nimmanhaemin or from the Night Bazaar to Chiang Mai Zoo.
Longer Trips (6-10 kilometers): 150 to 300 THB ($5 to $9 USD), typically for longer journeys, such as going from the Old City to Doi Suthep or other far-out attractions like the Elephant Nature Park.

Day Tours: Some tuk tuk drivers provide all-day tours, where they will drive you to multiple attractions. Prices for these tours usually range from 500 to 1,500 THB ($15 to $45 USD) for a half or full day, depending on the number of destinations and time involved.

How to Negotiate Fares

Negotiation is Key: It's common to negotiate the fare with tuk tuk drivers before you begin the journey. Always agree on the price before you set off to avoid misunderstandings.
Metered vs. Fixed Rates: Unlike taxis, most tuk tuks in Chiang Mai do not have meters, so fares are usually negotiated. However, if the driver is extending a fixed-rate tour, it's often more economical than paying per trip.
Consider Group Travel: If you're traveling with others, tuk tuks can be a more affordable way to get around, as the cost per person will be lower.

Tips for Riding Tuk Tuks

Be Prepared to Haggle: Don't be afraid to negotiate with drivers. You can often lower the price by extending a reasonable counter to their initial quote.

Safety First: While tuk tuks are fun, they can be a little bumpy and less secure than other forms of transportation. Always make sure you're seated comfortably and hold on during the ride.
Avoid Overpaying: For popular tourist routes, tuk tuk drivers may charge slightly more than for locals, so always check the price beforehand and be cautious of inflated fares.

Alternatives to Tuk Tuks

If you prefer a different mode of transport, Chiang Mai also provides other options such as:

Songthaews (red trucks), which are a great alternative for shared rides.
Grab (the Southeast Asian ridesharing app) for a more regulated, fixed-price option.
Bicycles and Scooters: Chiang Mai is a bike-friendly city, and renting a bike or scooter is another great way to get around.

Songthaews

What Are Songthaews?

A songthaew (meaning "two rows") is a shared taxi, typically a pickup truck with two long benches in the back for passengers. They are often red in Chiang Mai, but you may also see blue or other colors depending on the area. Songthaews operate on fixed routes, or they can be hired for private trips or tours.

Where to Find Songthaews

Main Streets and Tourist Areas: Songthaews are abundant around popular spots like the Old City, Nimmanhaemin Road, the Night Bazaar, and Chiang Mai University.

Flagging Down: You can flag down a songthaew on the street, or they can often be found waiting near major intersections or tourist spots.

Shared Rides or Private Hire: Songthaews can be shared with other passengers for a lower price, or you can hire the entire vehicle for a private ride to a specific destination.

Price Range

Songthaews usually have fixed fares for popular routes, but prices can vary depending on whether you're traveling a short or longer distance and whether it's a shared ride or a private hire. Here's an approximate breakdown of songthaew fares:

Short Trips (Within the City):

Price Range: 30 to 50 THB ($1 to $2 USD) per person for a short ride within the city, such as from the Old City to the Night Bazaar or Chiang Mai Gate.
Shared Ride: This is typically a shared ride, where you may have to wait for the vehicle to fill up with passengers before it departs.

Medium Distance Trips (3-5 kilometers):

Price Range: 50 to 100 THB ($2 to $3 USD) per person for trips like from the Old City to Nimmanhaemin Road or from the Night Bazaar to Chiang Mai Zoo.

Longer Distance Trips (6-10 kilometers):

Price Range: 100 to 200 THB ($3 to $6 USD) for longer rides, such as from the Old City to Doi Suthep or the Elephant Nature Park.

Private Hire for Short Trips:

Price Range: 200 to 500 THB ($6 to $15 USD) for private rides within the city, depending on the distance and negotiation.

Full-Day or Tour Packages:

Price Range: 1,000 to 2,000 THB ($30 to $60 USD) for a private songthaew for a day tour, such as visiting Doi Suthep, the Chiang Mai Zoo, and other attractions.

How to Use Songthaews

Flagging Down: To catch a songthaew, simply wave your hand at the vehicle when you see one passing by. If the vehicle is full or going in the wrong direction, it will continue on its way. Negotiating Fare: When taking a private ride, always negotiate the fare before getting in.

Agree on the price beforehand to avoid misunderstandings.
Shared Rides: If you're taking a shared ride, the songthaew will typically follow its route, picking up and dropping off passengers along the way. It's more affordable, but you may have to wait for it to fill up with passengers before it departs.

Advantages of Using Songthaews

Affordable: Songthaews are an inexpensive way to travel, especially for short trips within the city.
Flexible: You can either take a shared ride or hire a private vehicle for more convenience.
Local Experience: Riding a songthaew is a fun and authentic way to experience Chiang Mai's local culture.

Travel Tips for Using Songthaews

Negotiation is Key: For private hires, always agree on the price before starting your journey.
Check for Safety: Although songthaews are generally safe, be cautious when riding without seatbelts, as the open back can be a bit bumpy.
Patience for Shared Rides: If you're taking a shared songthaew, be prepared to wait a little

longer for other passengers to fill the vehicle before it departs.

Buses

1. City Buses

Chiang Mai has a limited number of city buses that run on fixed routes within the city. These are operated by Chiang Mai Public Transportation, and they connect key areas, including major shopping centers, bus terminals, and popular tourist spots.

Routes:

City buses have designated routes that generally cover popular locations, including:

Route 1: Chiang Mai Old City → Nimmanhaemin → Central Festival
Route 2: Old City → Chiang Mai Zoo → Huay Kaew Road
Route 3: Old City → Chiang Mai Bus Station → Central Airport Plaza

Bus Stops:

Buses have clearly marked stops along their routes, but you can also flag them down if you're in a visible area.

Price Range:

Single Journey Fare: 20 to 30 THB ($0.60 to $1 USD) per person, depending on the distance.
Day Pass: Some buses provide day passes or unlimited ride cards for tourists at around 100 to 150 THB ($3 to $5 USD), which can be used for travel within the city.

2. Minivans (Vans)

For intercity travel, minivans (also referred to as vans) are a popular and efficient way to travel between Chiang Mai and other cities or tourist destinations in northern Thailand.

Popular Routes:

Chiang Mai → Pai
Chiang Mai → Chiang Rai
Chiang Mai → Lampang
Chiang Mai → Mae Hong Son

These minivans operate from various minivan stations in the city, with departures usually scheduled throughout the day.

Price Range:

Chiang Mai → Pai: 150 to 250 THB ($5 to $7 USD) per person for a 3-4 hour journey. Chiang Mai → Chiang Rai: 200 to 300 THB ($6 to $9 USD) per person for a 3-hour trip. Chiang Mai → Mae Hong Son: 200 to 300 THB ($6 to $9 USD) per person for a 4-5 hour trip.

3. Private Bus Hire

For larger groups, private bus hire can be an affordable way to get around Chiang Mai or take a tour outside the city. Private buses are commonly used for group tours to attractions like Doi Suthep, the Elephant Nature Park, or the Golden Triangle.

Price Range:

Private Hire (Full-Day Tour): Around 2,500 to 5,000 THB ($75 to $150 USD) for a full-day hire, depending on the number of passengers and the route.

How to Use Buses in Chiang Mai

City Buses: You can board a city bus at the designated bus stop or flag it down along the route. Fares are paid in cash directly to the driver when you board.

Minivans: For intercity minivans, tickets can typically be purchased at the departure station or from travel agencies. It's recommended to buy tickets in advance for popular routes, especially during peak tourist seasons.

Advantages of Using Buses

Affordable: Buses are a cost-effective mode of transportation, especially for longer journeys or intercity trips.

Comfortable for Long Journeys: Minivans and buses provide a more comfortable experience for trips outside Chiang Mai, with air conditioning and better seating than tuk tuks or songthaews.

Access to Various Locations: Both city buses and intercity buses provide access to many key locations within and outside Chiang Mai.

Travel Tips for Using Buses

Check Schedules: City buses operate on set schedules, but minivan schedules may vary depending on demand and weather conditions. It's best to confirm departure times with the station or driver.

Advance Booking for Long-Distance Buses: For minivan trips to nearby cities like Pai or Chiang Rai, it's recommended to book tickets in advance, especially during high seasons (November to February).

Comfort: City buses can get crowded, especially during peak times (morning and late afternoon). If possible, avoid the busiest hours to have a more comfortable ride.

Luggage: If you're taking an intercity minivan, ask if there is space for luggage. Most services allow small bags, but larger items may need to be stored in the rear of the van.

Renting a Scooter or Bicycle

Renting a Scooter

Scooters are the most common form of transport in Chiang Mai, and many tourists opt to rent one for their convenience. The city is relatively easy to navigate with a scooter, and it's a great way to get to attractions outside the city center, such as Doi Suthep and the Elephant Nature Park.

Requirements:

Driver's License: You must have a valid motorcycle license to rent a scooter. International driving permits (IDP) are recommended for foreign travelers, especially for those from countries that have an agreement with Thailand.

Safety Gear: Helmets are mandatory by law, and most rental agencies will provide one when you rent the scooter.

Price Range:

Daily Rental: 150 to 300 THB ($4 to $9 USD) per day for a standard scooter.
Weekly Rental: 1,000 to 2,000 THB ($30 to $60 USD) per week for a longer rental.
Monthly Rental: 3,000 to 5,000 THB ($90 to $150 USD) per month, depending on the scooter's model and condition.

Types of Scooters Available:

Standard Scooters: Honda Click, Yamaha Fino, or similar models. These are ideal for short trips within the city and around town.
Larger Scooters: Honda PCX, Yamaha Nmax, or larger motorbikes may be available for those looking for more power for trips outside the city or up the mountains.

Where to Rent:

Rental Agencies: Numerous agencies around the Old City, Nimmanhaemin Road, and the Night Bazaar provide scooter rentals. Look for places with good reviews and proper insurance options.

Hotels and Guesthouses: Many hotels and guesthouses in Chiang Mai also rent scooters, though prices may be a little higher than independent rental shops.

Tips for Renting a Scooter:

Inspect the Scooter: Before renting, inspect the scooter for damage and take photos to avoid being charged for pre-existing issues when you return it.

Insurance: Consider paying extra for insurance, as accidents can happen. Make sure the insurance covers theft and damages.

Traffic: Be mindful of local driving laws and traffic patterns. Chiang Mai can be chaotic at times, especially around rush hour, so always drive defensively.

Parking: Be cautious about where you park your scooter, as some areas might have strict rules, and fines can be imposed for illegal parking.

Renting a Bicycle

Types of Bicycles Available:

Standard Bicycles: These are simple, no-frills bicycles, perfect for short city trips and easy sightseeing.
Mountain Bicycles: Great for outdoor adventures, including trips to Doi Suthep or along rural routes outside the city.
Electric Bikes: Some rental shops also provide e-bikes for a more comfortable ride with less effort, especially useful for hilly terrain.

Price Range:

Daily Rental: 50 to 150 THB ($1.50 to $5 USD) per day for a standard bicycle.
Electric Bike Rental: 300 to 500 THB ($9 to $15 USD) per day for an electric bike.

Weekly Rental: 300 to 700 THB ($9 to $21 USD) for a regular bike, depending on the type and quality.
Monthly Rental: 1,500 to 2,500 THB ($45 to $75 USD) for a longer-term rental.

Where to Rent:

Bike Rental Shops: These can be found throughout the city, especially near the Old City, Nimmanhaemin, and the Night Bazaar. Some specialized shops provide guided cycling tours as well.
Hotels and Guesthouses: Many hotels provide bicycles for rent, often at a slightly higher rate.

Tips for Renting a Bicycle:

Safety: Always wear a helmet (some rental shops may provide them for free or for a small fee) and use lights if cycling in the evening.
Cycling Routes: The Old City is very bike-friendly, and you can also cycle along the Ping River or out to nearby parks. Be cautious when riding in traffic, as roads can be busy.

Lock and Secure: Bicycles should be locked whenever left unattended. It's advisable to rent a good quality lock to ensure the bike stays safe while you visit attractions.

Advantages of Renting a Scooter or Bicycle

Flexibility: Renting a scooter or bicycle gives you the freedom to explore at your own pace, without being reliant on taxis, tuk tuks, or public transport.

Cost-Effective: Both options are affordable, and renting for multiple days can save you money compared to other modes of transport.

Local Experience: Riding a scooter or bicycle lets you experience Chiang Mai like a local, whether you're exploring the city's streets or venturing into the countryside.

Safety and Travel Tips

Wear a Helmet: It's the law, and safety should always be your priority, especially in traffic-heavy areas.

Traffic Awareness: Chiang Mai's traffic can be chaotic at times. Always follow local road rules and be mindful of other vehicles, especially on busy roads.

Keep Your Belongings Safe: Avoid leaving valuables on your scooter or bicycle when you park. Use a lock or take your belongings with you.

Navigating Chiang Mai with Sharing Apps

Using Ride-Hailing Apps (Grab, Bolt)

Grab

Grab is the most widely used ride-hailing service in Chiang Mai, extending a range of options from taxis to private cars and motorcycles. It's known for being reliable and easy to use, especially for those who prefer a cashless and hassle-free experience.

How to Use Grab:

Download the App: Grab is available for both iOS and Android. Simply download the app from your app store and sign up.

Enter Your Destination: Once logged in, type your pickup and drop-off locations. Grab will show you available ride options based on your location.

Select Ride Type: Grab provides various types of rides, including GrabCar (private car), GrabBike (motorbike), and GrabTaxi.

Payment: Grab supports both cash and cashless payments through credit/debit cards or mobile wallets.

Bolt

Bolt is another popular app in Chiang Mai, similar to Grab, providing rides with a few taps on your smartphone. It is gaining popularity and is often a cheaper alternative to Grab for rides within the city.

How to Use Bolt:

Download the App: Bolt is available for both iOS and Android.

Enter Your Pickup Location and Destination: Just like Grab, input your starting point and where you want to go.

Choose Your Ride Type: Bolt provides economy rides as well as premium options.

Payment: Bolt also allows cashless payments via credit cards or mobile wallets.

Price Range for Ride-Hailing Apps:

The price of a ride using apps like Grab and Bolt depends on the distance, time of day, and traffic conditions. However, you can typically expect the following price ranges:

Grab or Bolt Ride within the City (Short Distance):
Price Range: 50 to 100 THB ($1.50 to $3 USD) for short trips like from the Old City to the Night Bazaar or Nimmanhaemin Road.

Grab or Bolt Ride for Medium Distance (3-5 kilometers):
Price Range: 100 to 150 THB ($3 to $4.50 USD) for trips such as from the Old City to Doi Suthep or Chiang Mai Zoo.

Grab or Bolt for Longer Distance (6-10 kilometers):

Price Range: 150 to 250 THB ($4.50 to $7.50 USD) for longer trips, including destinations like the Elephant Nature Park or Chiang Mai Airport.

GrabBike or Bolt Motorcycle:

Price Range: 30 to 80 THB ($1 to $2.50 USD) for short motorcycle rides, which can be a faster and more affordable way to avoid traffic, especially during rush hours.

Benefits of Using Sharing Apps in Chiang Mai

Convenience: With just a few taps on your phone, you can easily request a ride from anywhere in the city and get picked up at your location, eliminating the need to hail a taxi or wait for a tuk tuk.

Cashless Transactions: You can pay for your ride using a credit card or mobile wallet, avoiding the need to carry cash and reducing the chances of dealing with inaccurate fare negotiations.

Language Barrier: The app's interface is in English, making it easier for foreign tourists to communicate their destinations without worrying about language barriers with drivers.

Safety: Both Grab and Bolt provide driver ratings and reviews, allowing you to choose reputable drivers, and in the case of Grab, you can also share your trip details with a friend for added security.

Real-Time Pricing: The app shows the estimated fare for your ride upfront, allowing you to see the cost before confirming your trip, which makes it easier to budget your travel expenses.

Travel Tips for Using Sharing Apps

Check Traffic and Timing: During rush hours (morning and evening), traffic can be heavy in Chiang Mai, especially in popular areas like the Old City and Nimmanhaemin. Prices may be higher during these times due to traffic congestion.

Confirm Ride Details: Before getting into a vehicle, confirm the car's make, model, and license plate number with the app to ensure you're getting into the right vehicle.

Plan for Airport or Longer Trips: For airport transfers or trips to more distant locations like Doi Suthep, it's better to use ride-hailing apps with fixed pricing so that you're not subject to potential fare hikes.

Motorbike Option: If you're in a rush or want to avoid traffic, GrabBike or Bolt motorcycles are a quick and budget-friendly alternative to traditional cars. They can be especially useful in Chiang Mai's busy downtown areas.

Other Ride-Sharing Apps

Besides Grab and Bolt, other smaller or local ride-hailing services may be available in Chiang Mai, though their availability may vary. It's worth checking your app store for regional services that cater specifically to northern Thailand.

ACCOMMODATION

Best Areas to Stay

Old City

The Old City of Chiang Mai is one of the most popular and iconic places to stay for first-time visitors. Surrounded by ancient walls and a moat, this historical district is a charming mix of traditional temples, vibrant markets, and cozy cafes, making it an ideal base for exploring the city. Staying in the Old City provides easy access to some of Chiang Mai's most famous attractions, such as Wat Phra Singh, Wat Chedi Luang, and the Sunday Walking Street Market. It's also close to a variety of restaurants, street food stalls, and lively entertainment options.

Why Stay in the Old City?

Central Location: The Old City is located in the heart of Chiang Mai, with many of the city's major landmarks and cultural sites within walking distance.
Historical Charm: The area is full of beautiful old temples, ancient city gates, and traditional Lanna architecture, providing a unique

atmosphere for those interested in history and culture.

Great for First-Time Visitors: With its central location and proximity to major tourist attractions, the Old City is perfect for those who want to experience the best of Chiang Mai in a short amount of time.

Vibrant Atmosphere: The Old City is bustling with life, extending plenty of local food, markets, and street vendors, making it ideal for travelers who want to be immersed in the local culture.

What to Expect in the Old City

Temple Visits: The Old City is home to some of Chiang Mai's most famous and beautiful temples. Don't miss visiting Wat Phra Singh, Wat Chedi Luang, and Wat Chiang Man. Many of these temples provide peaceful courtyards, historical architecture, and the chance to experience Chiang Mai's spiritual side.

Markets and Shopping: The Old City is famous for its night markets and street markets, particularly the Sunday Walking Street Market (Sunday night), where you can find local crafts, clothing, art, and delicious street food.

Cafes and Restaurants: The area is full of cafes, restaurants, and food stalls, where you can sample authentic Northern Thai dishes like khao soi (a coconut curry noodle soup) and sai ua (Northern Thai sausage).

Peaceful Environment: While the Old City is lively, it still retains a laid-back, peaceful vibe, particularly around the ancient temples, where you can relax and take in the serene atmosphere.

Best Hotels and Accommodation in the Old City

The Old City provides a variety of accommodation options, from budget hostels to boutique hotels, to mid-range and luxury stays. Here are some options across different price ranges:

Budget Accommodation:

Green Tiger House: A cozy guesthouse with a relaxed atmosphere, located just a short walk from major temples. Rooms are clean, affordable, and come with basic amenities. Price range: 500–1,000 THB ($15–$30 USD) per night.
The Old City Hostel: A budget-friendly, social hostel with a great location in the heart of the Old City. Perfect for solo travelers and those

looking to meet others. Price range: 250–500 THB ($7.50–$15 USD) per night for a dormitory bed.

Mid-Range Accommodation:

Rachamankha: A stunning boutique hotel that combines luxury with traditional Lanna architecture. It provides spacious rooms, a beautiful pool, and is located within walking distance of the city's top attractions. Price range: 2,000–3,500 THB ($60–$100 USD) per night.
Tamarind Village: A tranquil, beautifully decorated hotel extending comfortable rooms, a relaxing garden, and a swimming pool. Located near the Sunday Walking Street Market, it's perfect for those wanting to stay in a central, peaceful area. Price range: 2,500–4,500 THB ($75–$135 USD) per night.

Luxury Accommodation:

Four Seasons Resort Chiang Mai: While located just outside the Old City, this luxury resort provides a peaceful retreat with a stunning view of the surrounding mountains, luxurious villas, and world-class amenities. Price range:

10,000–20,000 THB ($300–$600 USD) per night.

Anantara Chiang Mai Resort: A stylish riverside resort located just outside the Old City, extending modern luxury with traditional Thai charm. The resort is perfect for travelers who want to enjoy luxury and tranquility while being close to the Old City's attractions. Price range: 6,000–12,000 THB ($180–$360 USD) per night.

Nearby Attractions

Staying in the Old City means you'll have easy access to a wide range of attractions. Here are some must-visit sites:

Wat Phra Singh: One of the most famous temples in Chiang Mai, featuring beautiful Lanna architecture and a peaceful atmosphere.
Wat Chedi Luang: Known for its towering ancient chedi, this temple provides a glimpse into Chiang Mai's history and spiritual life.
Chiang Mai City Arts and Cultural Centre: A great place to learn about the history and culture of Chiang Mai.
Sunday Walking Street Market: A must-see if you're in town on a Sunday. It's the perfect

place to shop for unique souvenirs and enjoy local food and performances.

Tha Phae Gate: The historic main entrance to the Old City, extending a glimpse of Chiang Mai's past.

Travel Tips for Staying in the Old City

Noise Levels: While the Old City is relatively peaceful, certain areas near the markets or temples can get busy, especially in the evenings or on weekends. Choose accommodation near quieter streets if you prefer a more tranquil stay.

Get Around by Foot or Bike: The Old City is small and walkable, so it's easy to explore on foot or by bike. Many hotels provide bicycle rentals.

Street Food: Be sure to try the street food around the Old City, especially near the markets. Local favorites include mango sticky rice, khao soi, and pad thai.

Dress Modestly for Temples: When visiting temples, ensure you dress modestly, covering your shoulders and knees as a sign of respect.

Nimmanhaemin

Nimmanhaemin, often simply called "Nimman," is a trendy, cosmopolitan neighborhood located west of Chiang Mai's Old City. Known for its vibrant atmosphere, modern cafes, upscale boutiques, and art galleries, Nimmanhaemin is a popular area for both expats and tourists looking for a lively yet more contemporary side of Chiang Mai. The area also provides a fantastic selection of restaurants, bars, and shopping options, making it a great choice for travelers who want a mix of modern amenities and local charm.

Why Stay in Nimmanhaemin?

Vibrant, Modern Atmosphere: Nimmanhaemin is one of the most dynamic neighborhoods in Chiang Mai, extending a wide variety of places to eat, shop, and relax. If you enjoy a lively urban atmosphere with plenty of modern comforts, Nimman is the place to be.

Great for Digital Nomads: The area is popular with digital nomads and expats due to its abundance of coworking spaces, reliable Wi-Fi, and excellent coffee shops, making it ideal for those who need to work remotely while exploring the city.

Food and Nightlife: Nimmanhaemin has a great food scene, with a variety of international and local restaurants, cafes, and street food options. The neighborhood also has a vibrant nightlife, with trendy bars and live music venues.

Proximity to Nature: While Nimman is known for its urban vibe, it's still located near some of Chiang Mai's natural attractions, including Doi Suthep and the Royal Park Rajapruek, making it a good balance of city life and nature.

What to Expect in Nimmanhaemin

Trendy Cafes and Restaurants: Nimman is home to some of Chiang Mai's best cafes, extending a mix of specialty coffee, delicious desserts, and international cuisine. Many places have beautiful interiors, ideal for both relaxation and work. Look out for popular spots like Ristr8to for coffee and The Salad Concept for healthy food options.

Boutiques and Shopping: The area is lined with boutiques, art galleries, and design stores extending everything from handmade jewelry to contemporary art. Maya Lifestyle Shopping

Center is a popular mall in the area, featuring international brands, a cinema, and restaurants.

Art and Culture: Nimman is also home to the Chiang Mai Art Museum and is near several independent galleries showcasing local contemporary art. The area has a creative, artistic vibe that appeals to visitors who appreciate art and culture.

Co-Working Spaces: Nimman is one of the top areas for digital nomads, with numerous coworking spaces like Punspace, Camp Chiang Mai, and Mueang Chiang Mai Co-Working Space.

Best Hotels and Accommodation in Nimmanhaemin

Budget Accommodation:

The Green Oasis: A budget-friendly guesthouse with clean, simple rooms located close to Nimman's cafes and shops. Ideal for budget-conscious travelers. Price range: 400–800 THB ($12–$25 USD) per night.

BED Nimman: A stylish and affordable boutique hotel extending great comfort and a central location near Nimman's vibrant street life. Price range: 800–1,500 THB ($25–$45 USD) per night.

Mid-Range Accommodation:

Hemp Chiang Mai: A charming and eco-friendly boutique hotel, extending stylish rooms and a serene atmosphere. It's located in a quieter area of Nimman but still within easy reach of the neighborhood's hotspots. Price range: 2,000–3,500 THB ($60–$105 USD) per night.
Hotel M Chiang Mai: A chic, modern hotel extending stylish rooms, a rooftop pool, and easy access to Nimman's cafes and bars. Perfect for travelers looking for a mix of relaxation and city vibes. Price range: 2,500–4,000 THB ($75–$120 USD) per night.

Luxury Accommodation:

Akyra Manor Chiang Mai: A luxury boutique hotel with a sophisticated design and exceptional service. extending spacious suites, rooftop dining, and a great location in the heart of Nimman. Price range: 5,000–10,000 THB ($150–$300 USD) per night.
Siri Lanna Hotel: A luxury hotel with Lanna-style architecture, extending large

rooms, a beautiful pool, and excellent amenities. It's a peaceful oasis with easy access to Nimman's entertainment and dining scene. Price range: 5,000–8,000 THB ($150–$240 USD) per night.

Nearby Attractions

Staying in Nimman puts you within easy reach of several attractions in Chiang Mai:

Doi Suthep: A must-see, Doi Suthep is one of the most iconic temples in Thailand, extending stunning views of the city from the mountain top. It's just a short drive from Nimman.

Chiang Mai Zoo: Located near Nimman, the Chiang Mai Zoo provides a relaxing visit with a variety of animals and beautiful scenery. The zoo also has a large aquarium and the famous Doi Suthep-Pui National Park.

Royal Park Rajapruek: A tranquil park with beautiful gardens and the Royal Pavilion, perfect for nature lovers and those looking to relax in a peaceful environment.

Maya Lifestyle Shopping Center: A modern mall with a variety of shops, restaurants, and a cinema, ideal for an afternoon of shopping and entertainment.

Art in Paradise: An interactive 3D art museum where you can pose and take photos with optical illusion artwork. A fun experience for families and anyone interested in unique art installations.

Travel Tips for Staying in Nimmanhaemin

Get Around by Foot or Bike: Nimman is a walkable neighborhood, and many of its attractions, cafes, and shops are within walking distance. If you want to explore farther, renting a bike is a great option, as the area is bike-friendly.

Be Ready for Traffic: While Nimman is a lively and central area, it can get quite busy, especially on weekends. Traffic around Soi 6 and the Nimmanhaemin Road can be congested, so try to plan your activities around peak traffic hours.

Nightlife: Nimman has a thriving nightlife scene, especially around Soi 7 and Soi 9. Whether you're into craft cocktails, live music, or laid-back pubs, there's something for every taste.

Weather Considerations: Like the rest of Chiang Mai, Nimman can get hot and humid, especially during the hot season (March–May).

Make sure to stay hydrated and wear comfortable clothing when exploring the area.

Riverside

The Riverside area of Chiang Mai is a peaceful and picturesque neighborhood located along the banks of the Ping River. This part of the city provides a more serene and scenic atmosphere, ideal for travelers seeking a tranquil escape while still being close to Chiang Mai's attractions. Known for its luxury hotels, riverside dining, and relaxed ambiance, the Riverside area is perfect for those who enjoy nature, beautiful views, and a more laid-back experience.

Why Stay in Riverside?

Scenic Beauty: The Ping River provides stunning views, particularly at sunrise and sunset. Many riverside hotels and restaurants provide outdoor seating where guests can enjoy the view while dining or relaxing.

Relaxed Atmosphere: The Riverside area is quieter and less hectic than the bustling Old City or Nimmanhaemin. It's perfect for those who want a peaceful environment to unwind after a day of sightseeing.

Luxury Accommodation: Riverside is home to some of Chiang Mai's most luxurious hotels and resorts, often featuring beautiful riverfront locations, stunning architecture, and top-tier amenities.

Proximity to Attractions: While the area is peaceful, it's still close enough to the Old City and Nimman for easy access to popular attractions, shopping, and dining.

What to Expect in Riverside

Riverside Dining: Many restaurants along the Ping River provide al fresco dining with beautiful views of the water and surrounding nature. Enjoy authentic Thai cuisine or international dishes while watching the sunset over the river. Popular spots include The Riverside Bar & Restaurant and Deck 1.

Peaceful Ambiance: Riverside is one of the quieter parts of the city, extending a calm and relaxing atmosphere ideal for nature lovers. The sound of the river and lush green surroundings create a perfect backdrop for a relaxing holiday.

Boat Tours: A popular activity in the Riverside area is taking a boat tour along the Ping River, extending a unique perspective of the city and surrounding nature. Many companies provide boat rides ranging from short trips to longer excursions.

Art and Culture: The Riverside area also has a number of cultural attractions, such as the Chiang Mai Arts and Cultural Center and Wat Chai Mongkhon (an important Buddhist temple along the river).

Best Hotels and Accommodation

Budget Accommodation:

Riverside Guesthouse: A simple, affordable guesthouse located along the river with basic amenities and comfortable rooms. Perfect for travelers who want a budget-friendly option with a peaceful riverside setting. Price range: 400–800 THB ($12–$25 USD) per night.
Baan Orapin: A charming guesthouse located by the Ping River, extending peaceful surroundings, comfortable rooms, and a relaxed atmosphere. Price range: 800–1,500 THB ($25–$45 USD) per night.

Mid-Range Accommodation:

Ping Nakara Boutique Hotel & Spa: A stylish and relaxing boutique hotel with a mix of modern and colonial-style design. Located near the river, it provides excellent amenities, a spa, and a great atmosphere. Price range: 2,000–4,000 THB ($60–$120 USD) per night. The Rim Chiang Mai: A beautiful hotel located near the river, extending spacious rooms and an outdoor pool. It's a good choice for those seeking a blend of comfort and tranquility, with easy access to the city's main attractions. Price range: 2,500–4,500 THB ($75–$135 USD) per night.

Luxury Accommodation:

Anantara Chiang Mai Resort: This 5-star luxury resort is situated along the Ping River and provides elegant rooms, beautiful river views, a world-class spa, and excellent dining options. It's the perfect retreat for those seeking luxury and peace. Price range: 8,000–15,000 THB ($240–$450 USD) per night.
Riverside House: A luxury riverside hotel that provides spacious, high-end rooms, a stunning riverfront location, and top-notch services. With direct access to the river, it's an ideal spot for travelers who want a tranquil stay with

upscale amenities. Price range: 6,000–12,000 THB ($180–$360 USD) per night.

Nearby Attractions

Staying along the Riverside means you're within reach of several important cultural and natural attractions:

Wat Chai Mongkhon: A beautiful and historic temple along the Ping River, known for its serene atmosphere and impressive architecture.

Baan Tawai Village: A short drive from the Riverside area, this village is famous for its traditional wooden handicrafts and art. It's an ideal place to shop for souvenirs and support local artisans.

Chiang Mai Night Bazaar: Located a short distance from the Riverside area, the Night Bazaar is a must-visit for those looking to shop for local crafts, clothing, and souvenirs, as well as sample street food.

Chiang Mai National Museum: Located near the Riverside area, this museum provides exhibits on the history, art, and culture of Chiang Mai and northern Thailand.

Boat Tours on the Ping River: Explore the river on a long-tail boat and experience the beauty of the surrounding countryside. Many companies provide boat rides that provide a unique view of the city from the water.

Travel Tips for Staying

Best for Peace and Relaxation: Riverside is the ideal area for travelers who prefer a quiet stay, but still want to be within reach of the city's main attractions. If you enjoy peaceful surroundings and river views, this is a perfect area to stay.

Transportation: While the Riverside area is more peaceful, it is a bit further from the nightlife and shopping of Nimman and the Old City. Taxis or tuk-tuks are easily available, but you may want to rent a bike or scooter for easier access to other parts of the city.

Boating Season: The best time for boat tours along the Ping River is during the cooler months (November to February) when the weather is more comfortable for outdoor activities.

Dining by the River: Make sure to dine at one of the many riverside restaurants for the full experience. Many places provide dinner cruises along the river, allowing you to enjoy a meal while taking in the scenic views.

Weather Considerations: Riverside provides a beautiful setting, but keep in mind that Chiang Mai can get quite hot, especially during the summer months. It's best to visit between November and February for cooler temperatures.

Santitham

Santitham is a quiet, residential neighborhood located just north of Chiang Mai's Old City. This area provides a more local, authentic experience compared to the tourist-heavy parts of the city. Known for its peaceful ambiance, Santitham is an excellent choice for those looking for a mix of convenience, local culture, and affordable accommodation. It's also a great area for exploring Chiang Mai beyond the typical tourist spots while still being close to the city's major attractions.

Why Stay in Santitham?

Local Experience: Santitham is largely a residential area, meaning you'll get to experience Chiang Mai like a local. It's perfect for those who prefer to avoid the hustle and bustle of more tourist-centric areas like the Old City or Nimman.

Affordable Accommodation: Compared to the pricier neighborhoods, Santitham provides budget-friendly hotels, guesthouses, and apartments, making it a good choice for travelers looking for good value.

Great Location: Santitham is conveniently located near the Old City, Nimmanhaemin, and other key areas, making it easy to get to popular attractions while staying in a quieter neighborhood.

Close to Local Markets: The area is home to a number of local markets and shops, providing an opportunity to sample traditional foods and purchase handmade goods at affordable prices.

Authentic Chiang Mai Vibe: Santitham is less commercialized and gives visitors a chance to enjoy the true spirit of Chiang Mai, with friendly locals, smaller family-owned businesses, and a slower pace of life.

What to Expect in Santitham

Residential Area with Local Shops: Santitham features traditional Thai houses and small shops, where you can find everything from local food to everyday items. It's a great place to get a feel for local life and experience the charm of Chiang Mai away from the crowds.

Affordable Dining: The area has a mix of small, affordable eateries, cafes, and street food vendors. Whether you're looking for a hearty Thai meal or a quick snack, Santitham has plenty of options for every budget. Don't miss trying the local specialties at the smaller, family-run restaurants.

Traditional Markets: Santitham is home to the Santitham Market, a great place to buy fresh produce, local snacks, and inexpensive clothing. The market provides a more authentic shopping experience compared to the tourist-heavy areas of the city.

Peaceful Ambiance: Santitham is quieter and less hectic than other parts of Chiang Mai, making it a great place to relax and unwind. The pace of life here is slow, extending a peaceful respite from the city's more tourist-driven areas.

Best Hotels and Accommodation

Budget Accommodation:

Green Tiger Vegetarian House: A budget-friendly guesthouse extending clean, comfortable rooms with a vegetarian-friendly menu. This guesthouse is popular with travelers who want a quiet place to stay while still being close to the action. Price range: 400–800 THB ($12–$25 USD) per night.

Santitham Guesthouse: A simple guesthouse with friendly service, located in a quieter part of Santitham. Perfect for budget travelers who want to be in a local neighborhood without paying a premium. Price range: 500–900 THB ($15–$30 USD) per night.

Mid-Range Accommodation:

Lae Nakhon Boutique Hotel: A comfortable boutique hotel in the Santitham area extending stylish rooms and a cozy atmosphere. The hotel is located near restaurants and markets, making it a great option for those wanting to explore local life. Price range: 1,500–2,500 THB ($45–$75 USD) per night.
The Empire Residence Nimman: Located on the edge of Santitham, this modern residence provides spacious rooms, a gym, and a relaxing atmosphere. It's ideal for travelers who want both comfort and access to nearby attractions. Price range: 2,000–3,500 THB ($60–$105 USD) per night.

Luxury Accommodation:

Awana Hotel Chiang Mai: A luxury hotel located on the edge of Santitham, extending large rooms, a pool, and excellent services. The hotel combines modern comforts with traditional Thai architecture, making it a peaceful retreat. Price range: 3,500–5,500 THB ($105–$165 USD) per night.

The Scent Hotel: A stylish boutique hotel extending a blend of modern and traditional design. It's located near Santitham and provides an upscale experience with a focus on personalized service. Price range: 4,500–7,000 THB ($135–$210 USD) per night.

Nearby Attractions

Staying in Santitham gives you access to both the Old City and nearby attractions:

Wat Chedi Luang: A historic temple located in the Old City, just a short distance from Santitham. The temple is home to a beautiful ancient chedi (stupa) and is a must-visit for those interested in Chiang Mai's rich history.

Chiang Mai Zoo: Located just south of Santitham, the zoo is a great family-friendly destination extending a variety of animals, as well as a large aquarium and a popular panda exhibit.

Nimmanhaemin Road: A short distance from Santitham, Nimman is a trendy area with cafes, restaurants, and shops. It's perfect for those looking for a more cosmopolitan experience while still being close to the local charm of Santitham.

Doi Suthep: Chiang Mai's most famous temple, Wat Phra That Doi Suthep, is located on a mountain just outside the city. It's easily accessible from Santitham and provides stunning views of the city below.

The Chiang Mai National Museum: Located near the northwestern edge of the Old City, this museum provides insight into Chiang Mai's history, culture, and art.

Travel Tips for Staying in Santitham

Perfect for Budget Travelers: Santitham is ideal for travelers on a budget who still want to stay in a peaceful neighborhood close to the city's attractions. Prices are generally lower than in more tourist-centric areas.

Getting Around: The area is well-connected to other parts of Chiang Mai by tuk-tuks, songthaews, and taxis. Renting a scooter or bicycle can be a good option to explore the area more freely.

Quiet Atmosphere: While Santitham is calm and quiet, it is still close to lively areas like Nimman and the Old City. If you're looking for a balance between local charm and easy access to Chiang Mai's main attractions, Santitham is an excellent choice.

Markets and Street Food: Make sure to visit Santitham Market and explore the local food stalls for authentic Thai dishes at low prices. This is one of the best ways to experience the local lifestyle.

Weather Considerations: The area, like the rest of Chiang Mai, can get quite hot in the summer months, so make sure to stay hydrated and wear light clothing. The best time to visit is from November to February when the weather is cooler.

Hotels

Luxury Hotels (3,500 – 10,000+ THB per night)

1. 137 Pillars House Chiang Mai

Description: A historic hotel extending luxurious suites, a serene atmosphere, and impeccable service.
Amenities: Spa, outdoor pool, fine dining restaurants.
Price Range: From 10,000 THB per night.

2. Shangri-La Chiang Mai

Description: A high-end hotel with spacious rooms, an outdoor pool, and world-class facilities.
Amenities: Spa, fitness center, multiple dining options.
Price Range: From 5,000 THB per night.

3. Anantara Chiang Mai Resort

Description: A stylish riverside resort known for its minimalist design, luxury spa, and scenic views.
Amenities: Infinity pool, wellness center, riverside dining.
Price Range: From 7,500 THB per night.

4. Four Seasons Resort Chiang Mai

Description: An opulent resort in the Mae Rim Valley, extending breathtaking views of rice paddies and mountains.

Amenities: Spa, yoga classes, cooking school.
Price Range: From 15,000 THB per night.

Mid-Range Hotels (1,000 – 3,500 THB per night)

5. U Chiang Mai

Description: A charming hotel in the Old City, known for its contemporary rooms and personalized service.
Amenities: Outdoor pool, fitness center, library.
Price Range: From 2,500 THB per night.

6. De Naga Hotel

Description: A boutique hotel located in the heart of the Old City, extending traditional Thai decor and modern comforts.
Amenities: Pool, spa, on-site restaurant.
Price Range: From 2,000 THB per night.

7. Eastin Tan Hotel Chiang Mai

Description: A modern hotel located near the trendy Nimmanhaemin area, ideal for shopping and dining.
Amenities: Indoor pool, gym, kids' club.
Price Range: From 3,000 THB per night.

8. Akyra Manor Chiang Mai

Description: A sleek, art-inspired hotel with a rooftop pool and bar, situated in the lively Nimmanhaemin neighborhood.
Amenities: Rooftop pool, fine dining, art gallery.
Price Range: From 3,500 THB per night.

Budget Hotels (Under 1,000 THB per night)

9. The Common Hostel

Description: A stylish and social hostel in the Old City, extending both private rooms and dorms.
Amenities: Shared kitchen, common area, free Wi-Fi.
Price Range: From 500 THB per night for dorm beds.

10. Raming Lodge Hotel & Spa

Description: A budget-friendly hotel located near the Night Bazaar, with traditional Thai interiors.
Amenities: Outdoor pool, spa, restaurant.
Price Range: From 800 THB per night.

11. BED Phrasingh Hotel

Description: A minimalist and highly-rated hotel close to Wat Phra Singh, known for its cleanliness and hospitality.
Amenities: Pool, free breakfast, 24-hour coffee and tea.
Price Range: From 1,000 THB per night.

12. Villa Duang Champa

Description: A cozy guesthouse with colonial-style architecture, located in the heart of the Old City.
Amenities: On-site cafe, garden area, live music events.
Price Range: From 900 THB per night.

Hostels

Social and Lively Hostels (200 – 500 THB per night)

1. Mad Monkey Hostel Chiang Mai

Description: A lively and social hostel with a great atmosphere for meeting fellow travelers. It features a pool and an on-site bar with nightly activities.
Amenities: Swimming pool, bar, tours and activities, free Wi-Fi.
Price Range: From 350 THB per night for dorm beds.

2. Bodega Chiang Mai Party Hostel

Description: Known for its vibrant party scene, this hostel provides a fun-filled experience with pub crawls, events, and social activities.

Amenities: Bar, nightly events, free breakfast, common lounge.
Price Range: From 300 THB per night for dorm beds.

3. Stamps Backpackers Hostel

Description: A sociable yet relaxed hostel extending pod-style dorm beds for added privacy. Great for meeting other travelers and participating in organized activities.
Amenities: Shared kitchen, movie nights, bike rentals, free Wi-Fi.
Price Range: From 250 THB per night for dorm beds.

Chill and Relaxed Hostels (150 – 400 THB per night)

4. The Entaneer Poshtel

Description: A clean and modern hostel with a cozy atmosphere, extending free breakfast and a helpful, friendly staff.
Amenities: Free breakfast, common area, bike rentals, travel desk.

Price Range: From 350 THB per night for dorm beds.

5. Green Sleep Hostel

Description: An eco-friendly and laid-back hostel in the Old City, with spacious dorm rooms and a focus on sustainability.
Amenities: Free breakfast, eco-friendly practices, comfortable common areas, free Wi-Fi.
Price Range: From 300 THB per night for dorm beds.

6. Deejai Hostel

Description: A relaxed hostel with a spacious garden and swimming pool, perfect for unwinding after a day of exploring.
Amenities: Pool access, communal kitchen, bar, chill-out areas.
Price Range: From 250 THB per night for dorm beds.

Boutique and Unique Hostels (250 – 600 THB per night)

7. Oxotel Hostel

Description: A stylish, industrial-designed hostel located near the Saturday Walking Street. It features a coffee shop and a mix of dorms and private rooms.
Amenities: On-site cafe, bike rentals, common lounge, air-conditioned rooms.
Price Range: From 400 THB per night for dorm beds.

8. The Common Hostel

Description: A sleek and modern hostel situated in the Old City, known for its cleanliness and comfortable beds. It's ideal for travelers looking for a more relaxed environment.
Amenities: Shared kitchen, free Wi-Fi, communal lounge, rooftop area.
Price Range: From 350 THB per night for dorm beds.

9. Hostel by BED

Description: A minimalist hostel that focuses on providing a good night's sleep with comfortable beds, free breakfast, and 24-hour coffee and tea.

Amenities: Free breakfast, unlimited bottled water, common area, laundry facilities.
Price Range: From 400 THB per night for dorm beds.

Budget-Friendly Hostels (100 – 250 THB per night)

10. Hug Hostel Rooftop

Description: A budget-friendly hostel with a fun rooftop bar, extending great views of the city and social events to meet other travelers.
Amenities: Rooftop bar, restaurant, bike rentals, free Wi-Fi.
Price Range: From 200 THB per night for dorm beds.

11. Slumber Party Hostel Chiang Mai

Description: A popular party hostel that provides daily events, pub crawls, and a fun, energetic vibe.
Amenities: Bar, events and tours, shared lounge, free Wi-Fi.

Price Range: From 180 THB per night for dorm beds.

Guesthouses

Budget-Friendly Guesthouses (200 – 800 THB per night)

1. Baan Klang Vieng

Description: A cozy and charming guesthouse located in the Old City, extending clean rooms and a peaceful courtyard.
Amenities: Free Wi-Fi, air-conditioned rooms, tour desk.
Price Range: From 500 THB per night.

2. Julie Guesthouse

Description: A popular choice for budget travelers, known for its relaxed vibe, garden area, and helpful staff. Great for socializing and meeting fellow travelers.

Amenities: On-site restaurant, bike rentals, common lounge.
Price Range: From 250 THB per night.

3. Chiang Mai Gate Capsule Hostel & Cafe

Description: A budget guesthouse extending capsule-style accommodations, perfect for travelers seeking a modern and affordable stay.
Amenities: On-site cafe, shared lounge, free Wi-Fi.
Price Range: From 300 THB per night.

4. Gap's House

Description: A peaceful guesthouse with lush gardens and traditional wooden architecture, located near Wat Phra Singh.
Amenities: Garden area, breakfast options, free Wi-Fi.
Price Range: From 400 THB per night.

Mid-Range Guesthouses (800 – 1,500 THB per night)

5. Rendezvous Guesthouse

Description: A centrally located guesthouse in the Old City, extending comfortable rooms and a rooftop terrace.
Amenities: Free Wi-Fi, rooftop terrace, travel services, air conditioning.
Price Range: From 1,000 THB per night.

6. Baan Bua Guesthouse

Description: A charming guesthouse surrounded by tropical gardens, ideal for those looking for a tranquil stay close to Chiang Mai's attractions.
Amenities: Garden views, air conditioning, breakfast options.
Price Range: From 900 THB per night.

7. Thapae Loft Guesthouse

Description: A stylish and modern guesthouse located near the Thapae Gate, with spacious rooms and a convenient location.
Amenities: Swimming pool, free Wi-Fi, on-site restaurant.
Price Range: From 1,500 THB per night.

8. Sri Pat Guesthouse

Description: A well-maintained guesthouse with a small outdoor pool, located in the heart of the Old City.
Amenities: Outdoor pool, free Wi-Fi, tour desk, bike rentals.
Price Range: From 1,200 THB per night.

Luxury Guesthouses (1,500 – 3,000 THB per night)

9. The Rim Chiang Mai

Description: A luxurious boutique guesthouse located at the edge of the Old City, extending elegant rooms and excellent service.
Amenities: Outdoor pool, fitness center, on-site restaurant.
Price Range: From 3,000 THB per night.

10. Yindee Stylish Guesthouse

Description: A chic and stylish guesthouse known for its beautifully designed rooms and prime location in the Old City.

Amenities: Free Wi-Fi, stylish interiors, common lounge area.

Price Range: From 1,800 THB per night.

11. Villa Duang Champa

Description: A colonial-style guesthouse with spacious rooms and a lovely balcony area overlooking the bustling streets of the Old City.

Amenities: On-site cafe, live music events, garden area.

Price Range: From 1,800 THB per night.

TOP ATTRACTIONS AND MUST-SEE SIGHTS

Doi Suthep

Location: Doi Suthep is a mountain located just to the west of Chiang Mai, approximately 15 km (9 miles) from the city center. It stands at an elevation of 1,676 meters (5,500 feet) above sea level.

Doi Suthep Temple (Wat Phra That Doi Suthep): The mountain is home to the Wat Phra That Doi Suthep, one of Thailand's most sacred and important Buddhist temples. The temple is a pilgrimage site for many Thais and provides stunning panoramic views of Chiang Mai.

Visiting Doi Suthep Temple (Wat Phra That Doi Suthep)

History: The temple was established in the 14th century and is deeply rooted in Thai Buddhism. According to legend, the temple was founded after a relic of the Buddha was placed on the back of a white elephant, which then climbed to the top of Doi Suthep, where it died. This was taken as a sign that the site was sacred, and the temple was built in its honor.

Main Attractions:

Golden Chedi: The central feature of the temple, the golden chedi (stupa), is adorned with intricate carvings and houses the Buddha's relic. Visitors can circle the chedi, making prayers and extending s.

Panoramic Views: The temple provides breathtaking views of Chiang Mai and the surrounding valleys. On clear days, you can see the entire city laid out below, surrounded by lush mountains.

Naga Serpent Staircase: A striking feature leading up to the temple, the 306-step staircase is flanked by beautifully crafted naga (serpent) sculptures. The climb to the temple is both spiritual and scenic.

The Temple's Surroundings: The temple grounds are serene, with lush gardens, smaller shrines, and statues that reflect the temple's importance in Thai religious life.

Other Attractions on Doi Suthep Mountain

Doi Suthep-Pui National Park: The mountain is part of the Doi Suthep-Pui National Park, which covers more than 260 square kilometers. The park is known for its lush forests, wildlife, and hiking trails.

Hiking Trails: One of the most popular hikes is the Monk's Trail, which leads from the base of the mountain up to Wat Phra That Doi Suthep, extending beautiful views of the surrounding forests and Chiang Mai.

Waterfalls: There are several waterfalls within the park, including the Huay Kaew Waterfall, located close to the base of the mountain. This is a lovely spot to relax and enjoy the nature surrounding Doi Suthep.

Hmong Hill Tribe Village: Near the top of the mountain, visitors can explore the Hmong Hill Tribe Village. This community provides a chance to learn about the Hmong culture, buy traditional crafts, and try local food.

How to Get to Doi Suthep

By Songthaew: One of the most common ways to reach the temple is by taking a songthaew (red truck). You can hire a songthaew from the city center, and it will take you to the base of Doi Suthep or directly to the temple, depending on the price you negotiate.

By Taxi: Taxis are another option, though they tend to be more expensive than songthaews.

By Motorbike: For more adventurous travelers, renting a motorbike is a great option. It provides flexibility, and the drive up the mountain is an enjoyable experience with beautiful scenery.

By Private Tour: Many tour operators provide day trips to Doi Suthep, often combined with visits to other nearby attractions. These tours typically include transportation and a guide.

By Car: If you're renting a car, the drive to Doi Suthep takes about 30-40 minutes from the city center. There is parking available at the base of the temple, and you can walk up the remaining steps or take a funicular ride.

Tips for Visiting Doi Suthep

Dress Modestly: As Doi Suthep is a sacred site, it's important to dress modestly. This means covering your shoulders and knees when entering the temple.

Best Time to Visit: The early morning or late afternoon is the best time to visit to avoid crowds and enjoy cooler temperatures. Sunrise and sunset also provide stunning views.

Bring Water: The hike or the drive up can be physically demanding, especially in the heat, so it's important to stay hydrated.

Respect the Temple: As with all religious sites in Thailand, be respectful of local customs and traditions. Quietly observe and take care when taking photos.

Why Visit Doi Suthep?

Cultural Significance: Wat Phra That Doi Suthep is one of Thailand's most revered temples and a symbol of Chiang Mai's spiritual heritage.

Scenic Views: The panoramic views from the temple and surrounding areas make it a photographer's paradise.

Natural Beauty: Doi Suthep is located in the heart of Doi Suthep-Pui National Park, extending lush forests, waterfalls, and hiking opportunities.
Local Experience: Visiting the Hmong Hill Tribe village provides insight into the unique culture and traditions of the hill tribes in northern Thailand.

Wat Phra Singh and Wat Chedi Luang

Wat Phra Singh

Location:
Located in the heart of Chiang Mai's Old City, just a short walk from Tha Phae Gate.

History and Significance:
Wat Phra Singh is one of the most important and revered temples in Chiang Mai. It was built in 1345 during the reign of King Pha Yu. The temple is named after the Phra Singh Buddha, a revered statue of the Buddha, which is believed to have been brought to Chiang Mai from Sri Lanka in the 14th century.

Phra Singh Buddha: This golden statue is one of the most sacred Buddha images in Thailand, housed inside the Viharn Lai Kham (Assembly Hall). It is believed to bring blessings and good fortune to worshipers and has a rich history tied to Chiang Mai's spiritual and royal past.

Key Features and Attractions:

1. Viharn Lai Kham: This is the main hall where the Phra Singh Buddha is enshrined. The hall's interior is known for its stunning Lanna-style architecture and intricate murals that depict Buddhist teachings.

2. Chedi: The temple's chedi (stupa) is an impressive example of the Lanna architectural style, with a golden spire that shines brightly under the sun. It houses the relics of important Buddhist figures.

3. Traditional Lanna Architecture: The temple complex is a beautiful example of Lanna architecture, featuring intricately carved wooden structures, gold leaf decorations, and ornate roofs.

4. Garden and Courtyards: Wat Phra Singh has well-maintained gardens and peaceful courtyards where visitors can meditate and enjoy the serene surroundings.

Cultural Importance:

The temple is an important site for the annual Songkran Festival (Thai New Year), where locals gather for traditional ceremonies. The temple also hosts various religious ceremonies and rituals throughout the year.

Wat Chedi Luang

Location:
Wat Chedi Luang is also located in Chiang Mai's Old City, just a short walk from Wat Phra Singh.

History and Significance:
Wat Chedi Luang was built in the 14th century during the reign of King Saen Muang Ma. It is renowned for its massive chedi (stupa), which was once the tallest structure in Chiang Mai.
The chedi was originally 82 meters tall, but earthquakes in the 16th century caused parts of it to collapse, leaving it in its current state. Despite its damaged state, the chedi remains a symbol of Chiang Mai's rich history and architectural prowess.

Key Features and Attractions:

1. Chedi: The massive, partially ruined chedi is the main feature of the temple complex. Visitors can admire the grandeur of the structure and see the detailed carvings of animals and mythical creatures along its base. The chedi once housed the Emerald Buddha (Thailand's most revered Buddha image) before it was moved to Bangkok.

2. Viharn: The temple's main hall, or viharn, is home to a revered Buddha statue. The hall is less ornate than the one at Wat Phra Singh, but it provides a quiet and reflective atmosphere.

3. Spirit Shrines: The temple grounds feature a collection of spirit shrines and statues, adding to the spiritual ambiance of the temple.

4. Monk Chats: Wat Chedi Luang is known for hosting monk chat sessions, where tourists can converse with Buddhist monks about their teachings and Thai culture. This is a unique opportunity for cultural exchange and learning.

Visiting Tips:

Evening Visit: Wat Chedi Luang is particularly striking at night when the temple is illuminated, and the atmosphere is more tranquil.
Respect the Monks: When engaging with monks, particularly during monk chats, always be respectful and follow proper etiquette. Women, for instance, should avoid physical contact with monks.
Admission Fee: There is a small entrance fee, which helps maintain the temple grounds.

Comparison of Wat Phra Singh and Wat Chedi Luang:

Why Visit Both?

Wat Phra Singh is ideal for those seeking a peaceful and spiritual atmosphere, along with a chance to admire Lanna-style architecture and artwork.

Wat Chedi Luang, with its grand yet partially ruined chedi, provides a glimpse into Chiang Mai's past grandeur and a chance to learn about the city's history and culture, especially through the monk chat sessions

Chiang Mai Old City and Its Ancient Walls

Chiang Mai Old City:
The Old City of Chiang Mai is the historic heart of the city, rich in culture, ancient architecture, and significant landmarks. It is a square-shaped area surrounded by moats and ancient walls, which once served as fortifications to protect the city from invasions. The Old City is where you can find some of Chiang Mai's most famous temples, traditional markets, and narrow lanes lined with quaint shops and guesthouses.

The Ancient Walls and Moats

The Old City is encircled by four square-shaped walls and a moat that were originally built in the late 13th century during the reign of King Mengrai, the founder of Chiang Mai. These walls and the moat were constructed as a defense mechanism to protect the city from external threats, including invasions by neighboring kingdoms. Though the original structure has been weathered and parts of it have disappeared over time, significant portions of the walls and moat still stand today, providing insight into the city's past.

Key Features of the Ancient Walls

1. The Four Main Gates:
The Old City's walls have four main gates, each located on one side of the city. These gates were the main entry points for travelers, traders, and armies, and they remain important landmarks today.
Tha Phae Gate: Located to the east, Tha Phae Gate is the most famous and iconic of the four gates. It is a popular starting point for visitors to Chiang Mai's Old City and is often used as a backdrop for photographs. The gate is beautifully restored and still retains much of its original charm.
Chiang Mai Gate: On the southern side, Chiang Mai Gate is known for its lively night market. This gate is smaller but still stands as a reminder of the city's past.
Suan Dok Gate: On the western side, this gate is less prominent but still plays a role in the city's history. Nearby, the Wat Suan Dok temple is a famous attraction.
Sampeng Gate: On the northern side, this gate is largely intact and was used as a major entrance to the city in the past. It's quieter and less frequented by tourists than Tha Phae Gate.

2. Moat:

The moat that runs around the Old City was an important part of the city's defense system. It served as a water source and provided additional protection against invaders. While the moat is not used for defensive purposes today, it remains a significant feature and is a lovely spot for a walk or bicycle ride around the Old City. Several bridges cross the moat, extending picturesque views of the city's traditional architecture.

3. Wall Remnants:

While the majority of the walls have been eroded or replaced with modern buildings, several portions of the ancient brick wall still stand, particularly near the main gates. These remnants of the wall provide a glimpse into the architectural style of the time and how the city's fortifications looked in the past.

Exploring Chiang Mai Old City

1. Walking Tour of the Walls:

One of the best ways to explore the Old City is to take a leisurely walking tour around the moat and the walls. Many visitors enjoy walking or cycling around the moat, stopping at key gates, and exploring the various temples and markets inside the Old City.

2. Temples and Landmarks:
The Old City is home to many of Chiang Mai's most famous temples, many of which are located near or within the city's ancient walls.
Wat Phra Singh and Wat Chedi Luang are two of the most famous temples in the Old City, both of which are easy to access and provide a chance to see Chiang Mai's rich cultural and religious heritage.
Wat Chiang Man, the oldest temple in Chiang Mai, also stands within the Old City walls.
Sunday Walking Street Market: This market takes place on Ratchadamnoen Road, which runs through the center of the Old City. It's one of the best places to experience local crafts, food, and culture.

3. City Parks and Gardens:
The Old City also features several parks and green spaces, including the Suan Buak Haad Park, a peaceful park near Chiang Mai Gate. The park is a great spot for relaxing after a walk around the walls.

4. Street Art:
In recent years, the Old City has also become home to street art, with murals and creative installations appearing on walls throughout the area. This modern art provides a contrast to the historic walls and temples, blending the old and new aspects of Chiang Mai's identity.

Chiang Mai Night Safari

Located just a short drive from the city center, the Chiang Mai Night Safari is a large wildlife park that covers an area of about 1,000 acres. It is divided into three main zones, each with its own distinct experience. The park allows you to explore the animal world after dark, showcasing a wide variety of species from around the world.

Main Zones of the Night Safari

1. Safari Tram Ride:

This is the main attraction of the Chiang Mai Night Safari. The tram ride takes visitors through different habitats where they can observe various animals in their natural, nocturnal setting. The tram is guided by a knowledgeable ranger who provides insights into the animals' behaviors and habits.

The tram passes through three distinct zones:

Savannah Safari: Home to animals like zebras, giraffes, antelopes, and wildebeests.
Predator Prowl: Features nocturnal predators such as lions, tigers, leopards, and cheetahs. The animals in this zone are often more active during the evening, making this part of the safari particularly exciting.
Night Safari Zone: A zone where visitors can see creatures that are typically active during the night, such as deer, wild boar, and various species of birds.

2. Walking Trail:

In addition to the tram ride, there's a walking trail that visitors can explore at their own pace. The trail is designed to give guests a more intimate experience with the animals, and it also features a variety of nocturnal species, such as owls, reptiles, and smaller mammals.
The walking trail is lit in some areas, ensuring that visitors can safely navigate while enjoying close encounters with the animals.

3. Special Animal Shows and Exhibitions:

The Night Safari features a variety of animal shows, including performances that showcase the skills and behaviors of the park's residents. These shows typically focus on animals' natural abilities, such as the hunting skills of predators and the acrobatics of certain birds and primates.
The shows are entertaining and educational, perfect for both adults and children.

Popular Animals to See at the Night Safari

The Chiang Mai Night Safari is home to a wide variety of species from around the world. Some of the most popular animals that visitors can expect to see include:

Big Cats: Lions, tigers, leopards, and cheetahs are some of the main attractions, especially in the Predator Prowl zone.
Giraffes and Zebras: These herbivores are often spotted grazing in the Savannah Safari zone.
Deer and Wild Boar: Common in the Night Safari Zone, these animals are most active in the evening hours.

Asian Elephants: The park also houses some Asian elephants, which are a symbol of Thailand's wildlife.

Bats, Owls, and Other Birds: The park has a variety of nocturnal birds, including owls, eagles, and other species.

Reptiles and Amphibians: The walking trail is a good spot to see reptiles such as snakes, turtles, and lizards.

Facilities and Services

Restaurants and Dining: The Night Safari has a variety of dining options, ranging from casual food stalls to more formal restaurants. Visitors can enjoy Thai and international cuisine while watching the animals in the background.

Gift Shop: Souvenirs, including animal-themed merchandise, can be purchased at the park's gift shop.

Kids' Play Zone: The Night Safari also features a play area for children, making it a family-friendly destination.

Photography: The safari is a fantastic place for wildlife photography, but visitors should note that flash photography is typically not allowed to avoid disturbing the animals.

Ticket Prices and Hours of Operation

Ticket Prices:
Prices vary depending on the type of experience (tram ride, walking trail, animal shows, etc.). On average, tickets range from around 300 to 800 THB per person. There may be additional fees for special activities or shows.

Operating Hours:
The Chiang Mai Night Safari is typically open from 6:00 PM to 10:00 PM daily. The tram rides and shows are generally scheduled throughout the evening, with the last tram ride departing shortly before closing time.

Getting to the Chiang Mai Night Safari

The Chiang Mai Night Safari is located about 12 km south of the city center, making it easily accessible by taxi or tuk-tuk. The journey usually takes around 20–30 minutes depending on traffic.
Many hotels in Chiang Mai also provide shuttle services to the Night Safari, so it's worth checking with your accommodation beforehand.

Tips for Visiting the Night Safari

1. Dress Comfortably: Since you'll be walking and potentially spending a few hours outside, wear comfortable clothes and shoes. It's also a good idea to bring a light jacket as the evenings can get cool.

2. Be Mindful of the Animals: Flash photography and loud noises can disturb the animals. Keep a respectful distance and avoid using a flash when taking photos.

3. Plan for Dinner: If you're planning to stay for a few hours, you might want to enjoy dinner at one of the on-site restaurants. This will also give you a chance to relax and enjoy the atmosphere between the different activities.

4. Check Show Schedules: The animal shows happen at specific times, so be sure to check the schedule to ensure you don't miss them.

Bo Sang Handicraft Village

Bo Sang Village is often referred to as the "Umbrella Village", due to its reputation for producing colorful, hand-painted paper umbrellas and other handcrafted items. The village is home to generations of artisans who have passed down their techniques for making these umbrellas, which are crafted from bamboo and sa paper (a type of mulberry paper), creating delicate yet durable items that are both functional and decorative.

The village's atmosphere is one of authenticity, with small workshops and storefronts dotting the streets, where visitors can watch the craftsmen at work, interact with them, and even purchase the beautiful creations.

What to See and Do in Bo Sang Village

1. Umbrella Making:

The highlight of Bo Sang is watching artisans craft the iconic paper umbrellas. The process is fascinating and involves several steps:

Bamboo Frame Creation: Bamboo is carefully bent and shaped to form the structure of the umbrella.

Sa Paper Application: Sheets of sa paper are attached to the bamboo frame. This paper is handmade and durable, often sourced from local farms.

Hand-Painting: After the frame is assembled, skilled artists hand-paint intricate designs on the paper, often featuring floral patterns, scenes of nature, or traditional Thai motifs. The colors are bright and vivid, making each umbrella a unique work of art.

Finishing Touches: The umbrellas are then dried, treated to be water-resistant, and trimmed.

Visitors can observe each of these stages in the various workshops throughout the village.

2. Other Handicrafts: While Bo Sang is best known for its umbrellas, the village also produces other traditional handicrafts, including:

Hand-painted fans: Similar to the umbrellas, these are made with sa paper and decorated with floral or nature-themed designs.

Wooden Crafts: The village also has artisans who specialize in creating wooden carvings and furniture.

Silk and Cotton Products: Some workshops provide handwoven silk and cotton items, such as scarves, bags, and cushions, often with traditional Thai designs.

3. Bo Sang Umbrella Festival:

One of the most popular times to visit Bo Sang is during the annual Bo Sang Umbrella Festival, which usually takes place in January. During this festival, the village comes alive with a vibrant display of colorful umbrellas and other handicrafts. The festival includes:

Parades: Locals and visitors gather to enjoy parades featuring beautifully decorated umbrellas, traditional dance performances, and music.

Craft Demonstrations: The streets are lined with booths where artisans display their techniques and provide products for sale.

Cultural Exhibitions: The festival is also a celebration of traditional Thai culture, with events showcasing local crafts, food, and performances.

4. Shopping for Souvenirs:

Bo Sang is a great place to purchase souvenirs. The village's shops provide a wide range of beautifully crafted items such as:
Painted Umbrellas: These come in various sizes and colors, perfect for use as home decor or as practical umbrellas.
Hand-painted Fans: These make great gifts or keepsakes, showcasing Thai artistry.
Traditional Thai Clothing: Visitors can find handwoven fabrics and garments with intricate patterns.
Wood Carvings and Pottery: Many shops sell finely crafted wooden items, including statues, home decor, and kitchenware.

How to Get to Bo Sang Village

By Car: The easiest way to reach Bo Sang from Chiang Mai is by car or taxi, which will take about 20-30 minutes. You can also rent a scooter or a bicycle for a more local experience.
By Songthaew: Public transport options like songthaews (red trucks) are available from Chiang Mai. You can hire a songthaew for a round-trip ride or catch one from Chang Phuak Gate or Tha Phae Gate.

By Tour: Many tour companies in Chiang Mai provide half-day or full-day tours to Bo Sang Village, often combined with other nearby attractions like San Kamphaeng Hot Springs.

Tips for Visiting Bo Sang Village

1. Wear Comfortable Shoes: Since you will be walking through the village and visiting multiple workshops, wear comfortable footwear.
2. Take Your Time: The village is small, and it's easy to spend a few hours exploring, so take your time to appreciate the craftsmanship and interact with the artisans.
3. Bring Cash: While some shops may accept credit cards, it's always a good idea to carry cash, especially when purchasing handicrafts from smaller vendors.
4. Respect the Artisans: If you're taking photos of the artisans at work, always ask for permission first and be respectful of their space.
5. Consider a Souvenir: The items made in Bo Sang are authentic, handcrafted goods, making them perfect souvenirs or gifts. A hand-painted umbrella or fan can be a beautiful and unique memento of your trip.

CULTURAL EXPERIENCES AND FESTIVALS

Loy Krathong and Yi Peng Lantern Festival

Loy Krathong Festival: The Festival of Lights

Loy Krathong is one of Thailand's most iconic festivals, celebrated nationwide but particularly beautifully in Chiang Mai. The festival takes place on the full moon night of the 12th lunar month (usually in November), marking the end of the rainy season and paying homage to the Water Goddess (Phra Mae Khongkha).

Traditions and Significance of Loy Krathong

Krathong: The central tradition of Loy Krathong involves the creation and floating of a krathong (a small, decorated boat made of banana leaves, flowers, candles, and incense). People float their krathongs in rivers, lakes, or canals as an extending to Phra Mae Khongkha, the goddess of water, asking for forgiveness for any misdeeds and seeking good luck for the future.

Symbolism: The act of floating the krathong symbolizes the letting go of negativity, bad luck, and past troubles. The candles and incense represent light, hope, and prayers for a brighter future.

Activities during Loy Krathong

Floating Krathongs: Throughout Chiang Mai, locals and visitors can be seen floating their krathongs in the Ping River and smaller canals. The scene is magical, with thousands of lit-up krathongs creating a glittering path along the water.

Temple Visits: Many people visit temples, especially Wat Phra Singh and Wat Chedi Luang, to participate in prayers, lighting candles, and making extending s to seek blessings for their lives.

Fireworks and Lanterns: The sky is often lit up with fireworks, while lanterns (known as khom loi) are released into the sky, creating a dazzling display of lights.

Yi Peng Lantern Festival: The Sky Lanterns of Chiang Mai

The Yi Peng Lantern Festival is a traditional celebration of the Lanna culture, which is specific to the northern region of Thailand, especially Chiang Mai. Yi Peng is closely associated with the Loy Krathong festival but is distinct due to the emphasis on sky lanterns (khom loi) and the Lanna-style rituals.

Traditions and Significance of Yi Peng

Khom Loi (Sky Lanterns): The most iconic part of Yi Peng is the release of thousands of sky lanterns into the night sky. These lanterns, made from rice paper and fueled by a small flame, are released into the sky as a way of paying respect to the Buddha and seeking good fortune. The release of these lanterns is a symbolic gesture of letting go of the past year's troubles and sins and making wishes for the future.

Lanna Heritage: Yi Peng is deeply rooted in the Lanna Kingdom's traditions, and it is celebrated with a strong sense of cultural pride. People light candles and incense as part of the ritual, and the streets are filled with Lanna-style performances, dances, and music.

Activities during Yi Peng

Sky Lantern Release: The release of khom loi into the sky is the highlight of Yi Peng. The most famous event takes place at the Chiang Mai International Exhibition and Convention Centre, where visitors and locals gather to release lanterns, creating a breathtaking spectacle. It's a moment of serenity and beauty, with thousands of glowing lanterns lighting up the dark sky.

Lanna Cultural Performances: Traditional Lanna music, dance, and ceremonies are held throughout the city, particularly in the Old City area and around the temples. The celebrations often include parades, where participants wear traditional Lanna costumes, and performances of traditional Thai music and dance.

Candle Lighting at Temples: Another significant activity is visiting temples, particularly Wat Phra That Doi Suthep, where large numbers of people gather to light candles and incense as extending s to the Buddha. The temples are beautifully illuminated during the festival.

When Do Loy Krathong and Yi Peng Take Place?

Loy Krathong: Takes place on the full moon night of the 12th lunar month, usually in November. The exact date varies from year to year based on the lunar calendar.

Yi Peng: This festival typically coincides with Loy Krathong, as it's celebrated during the same time, but Yi Peng is specifically tied to the full moon and the northern Lanna culture. The celebrations can last for several days, and the lantern release happens on the night of the full moon.

Where to Celebrate Loy Krathong and Yi Peng in Chiang Mai

1. The Ping River:

The Ping River is one of the most iconic places to float krathongs. The scene of thousands of krathongs drifting on the river under the moonlight is magical. Many people gather along the riverbanks to set their krathongs afloat, while vendors sell candles and incense.

2. Doi Suthep Temple:

For those wishing to experience the spiritual side of the celebrations, a visit to Wat Phra That Doi Suthep is essential. The temple is an important site during the festival, and the view of the city from the mountaintop at night, illuminated by lanterns, is simply unforgettable.

3. Chiang Mai International Exhibition and Convention Centre:

This venue is famous for hosting large-scale Yi Peng events, with thousands of lanterns released into the sky in a stunning show of lights.

4. Temples in the Old City:

Wat Phra Singh and Wat Chedi Luang are popular places to visit for candle lighting and other spiritual activities during both Loy Krathong and Yi Peng.

Tips for Visiting the Loy Krathong and Yi Peng Festivals

1. Book Accommodations Early: These festivals attract large crowds, so accommodations in Chiang Mai fill up quickly. Make sure to book your stay well in advance.

2. Arrive Early for Lantern Releases: The release of sky lanterns can get crowded, especially at the Chiang Mai International Exhibition Centre. Arrive early to secure a good spot and participate in the ceremony.

3. Respect the Traditions: While these festivals are joyful, they are also spiritual events. Be respectful when participating in rituals, such as floating krathongs or lighting candles.

4. Be Prepared for Crowds: Both festivals are popular with both locals and tourists, so expect crowded streets and markets. Be patient and enjoy the festive atmosphere.

5. Safety Considerations: If you are participating in the lantern release, be aware of safety precautions. Lanterns are hot and can be dangerous if not handled properly. Many events will have safety measures in place, but

always follow the instructions given by organizers.

Songkran Festival

Songkran is one of the most significant and exciting festivals in Thailand, celebrated annually from April 13th to 15th. Known for its massive water fights and vibrant celebrations, it marks the Thai New Year and is a time for family reunions, spiritual rituals, and community festivities. Chiang Mai, being one of the best places to experience Songkran, provides a truly unique and unforgettable experience.

The Significance of Songkran

Thai New Year: Songkran marks the traditional Thai New Year, which is based on the lunar calendar. The festival is deeply rooted in Buddhist traditions, with rituals meant to honor elders, ancestors, and the Buddha.

Water Festival: The most famous aspect of Songkran is the water fight. The act of pouring water over others is symbolic, representing purification and the washing away of bad luck from the past year. Water is believed to bring good fortune, and during Songkran, it is used to cleanse, bless, and refresh.

Respect for Elders: Songkran is also a time for families to gather and show respect to their elders. Younger generations visit the homes of older family members to provide gifts and perform the rod nam dam hua ceremony, where water is poured over the hands of elders as a sign of respect.

Songkran Celebrations

Chiang Mai is renowned for hosting one of the largest and most vibrant Songkran festivals in the country, and it is an event that attracts both locals and tourists. Here's what you can expect during Songkran in Chiang Mai:

Water Fights

Ratchadamnoen Road: The heart of the Songkran water fights in Chiang Mai takes place on Ratchadamnoen Road, where locals and tourists gather to douse each other with water. This main street in the Old City becomes a battlefield for water guns, buckets, and hoses, with participants ranging from families to groups of friends.

Songkran Parades: Throughout the festival, you'll witness colorful parades of traditional floats, often featuring Buddha images and locals in traditional Thai attire. The floats are often splashed with water, and people throw water at one another as the parade moves through the streets.

Water Stations: Throughout the city, there are designated water stations where people fill up their buckets and water guns. Locals set up sprinklers, and there are even water trucks that drive down the streets, dousing anyone in their path.

Cultural and Religious Ceremonies

Songkran in Temples: While the water fights are the most popular part of Songkran, there are also religious rituals and cultural events that take place. Locals visit temples to make extending s, pray, and pay respects. Some of the key temples to visit during Songkran include:
Wat Phra That Doi Suthep: A major pilgrimage site, where people go to make extending s and perform traditional ceremonies to honor the Buddha.

Wat Phra Singh: A stunning temple in the heart of the Old City, often hosting Buddhist ceremonies and prayers during Songkran.

Wat Chedi Luang: A significant historical temple in Chiang Mai, where people participate in traditional rituals and receive blessings from monks.

Rod Nam Dam Hua Ceremony: This ceremony involves pouring water over the hands of elders to show respect. It is a peaceful, spiritual aspect of Songkran and often takes place in homes or temples.

Traditional Thai Music and Dance

Folk Music: During Songkran, there are often performances of traditional Thai folk music, especially in the Old City and other cultural hubs of Chiang Mai. Local bands may perform traditional Lanna songs, accompanied by dances and performances.

Traditional Dancing: Many of the parades and celebrations feature traditional Thai dance, such as Ram Wong, where dancers wear beautiful costumes and perform in groups. It's a great opportunity to see Lanna culture come alive through music and dance.

Tips for Enjoying Songkran in Chiang Mai

1. Prepare for the Water Fight:

Be ready to get wet! Everyone, from children to adults, participates in the water fights. Wear clothes that dry easily, preferably light, quick-drying fabrics.
Consider wearing goggles and waterproof bags to protect your phone and camera from getting soaked.

2. Respect the Traditions: While the water fights are a lot of fun, Songkran is also a time for spiritual observance. Be respectful at temples and during traditional ceremonies. If you're taking part in the rod nam dam hua ceremony, do so with reverence.

3. Safety First:

Stay hydrated! The weather in Chiang Mai during Songkran can be hot, and you'll be running around in water, so make sure you drink plenty of water.
Watch out for slippery streets and puddles caused by all the water being thrown around.
Use sunscreen, as the hot sun can cause sunburn during the festival.

4. Avoid Certain Areas if You Prefer Peace: If you're not interested in participating in the water fights, it's best to avoid the busiest areas like Ratchadamnoen Road. The temples and quiet parts of the Old City will provide a more peaceful Songkran experience.

5. Join in the Fun: Songkran is a festival that encourages participation. Whether you're a tourist or a local, grab a water gun and get involved in the fun! It's a fantastic way to experience the joy and camaraderie that Songkran brings.

Where to Celebrate Songkran in Chiang Mai

1. Old City (Ratchadamnoen Road): This is the main hotspot for the water fights, where people gather to engage in massive water battles. It's the most famous area, but it's also the busiest and wettest.
2. Nimmanhaemin Road: If you want a more laid-back experience but still want to be part of the action, head to Nimmanhaemin, a trendy area with fewer crowds but still plenty of water-splashing fun.

3. Temples (Wat Phra That Doi Suthep, Wat Chedi Luang, Wat Phra Singh): For a more spiritual and reflective Songkran experience, visit the temples for ceremonies and prayers.

4. Chiang Mai's Riverside: The riverside area, particularly near the Ping River, provides a unique experience to witness traditional Songkran activities and the floating of extending s.

Traditional Thai Dance and Muay Thai Shows

Traditional Thai Dance

Traditional Thai Dance is an ancient form of artistic expression, rich with meaning and steeped in Buddhist and royal traditions. It's a fascinating display of graceful movements, colorful costumes, and intricate hand gestures that narrate stories from Thai history, mythology, and folklore.

Types of Thai Dance

1. Classical Thai Dance (Ram Thai):

Ram Thai is one of the most prominent types of traditional dance, often performed during royal ceremonies, religious festivals, and important events. The dance is slow, deliberate, and graceful, involving exquisite hand movements, and is often accompanied by traditional Thai music played on instruments such as the piphat (an ensemble of traditional Thai instruments). Court Dances: These dances originated in the royal courts of the Siamese monarchy and depict stories from Thai history, including legends, Hindu mythology, and Buddhist tales.

2. Folk Dances (Ram Wong):

Ram Wong is a more community-oriented folk dance, where people gather to dance in a circle. This dance is light-hearted and often performed during festivals like Songkran and Loy Krathong. It's lively and inclusive, with simple steps that everyone can join in on.
Regional Variations: Different regions of Thailand have unique folk dances. For instance, in northern Thailand (Chiang Mai's

region), you can see Lanna dance, which has more fluid and expressive movements.

3. Khon Dance:

The Khon dance is a traditional Thai masked dance that depicts scenes from the Ramakien (the Thai version of the Ramayana). This highly stylized dance is performed with elaborate costumes, and dancers wear intricate masks. It's a dramatic and expressive art form, representing gods, demons, and heroes.

Where to Experience Thai Dance in Chiang Mai

Khantoke Dinner Shows: One of the best places to experience traditional Thai dance is during a Khantoke dinner. This is a traditional northern Thai banquet where visitors are served various local dishes while enjoying live performances of traditional dance, music, and sometimes Muay Thai demonstrations. You can find Khantoke shows at venues such as:
Old Chiang Mai Cultural Center: Known for its evening Khantoke dinner shows, this venue provides a fantastic opportunity to experience Lanna-style dance performances along with delicious local cuisine.

Siam Elephant Chiang Mai: This venue combines cultural shows with elephant experiences, often showcasing traditional Thai dance.

Temples and Cultural Events: During major festivals or events, such as Loy Krathong or Songkran, traditional dance performances can also be seen in temples or as part of community celebrations.

Muay Thai Shows

Muay Thai, also known as Thai boxing, is Thailand's national sport and a martial art with a deep cultural significance. It is often referred to as the "Art of Eight Limbs" because it involves the use of fists, elbows, knees, and shins. Muay Thai has a long history, dating back centuries, and has been deeply embedded in Thai culture, not only as a sport but as a form of discipline and respect.

What to Expect from a Muay Thai Show

Muay Thai shows are an exciting and thrilling way to experience this traditional martial art, with live demonstrations of fighting techniques and sometimes even full-on matches between skilled fighters.

1. Demonstrations of Techniques:

Some shows begin with a demonstration of the basic techniques of Muay Thai, such as the clinching, knee strikes, and elbow strikes. This allows spectators to see the art and skill behind the sport before watching an actual match.

2. Live Fights:

Many Muay Thai shows feature live boxing matches. These matches are usually staged with experienced fighters, who engage in controlled but intense bouts. The fighters wear traditional Muay Thai shorts and may also perform the Wai Kru (a traditional dance and ritual performed before each fight to show respect to their trainers, family, and the sport itself).

The matches often include commentary, and the audience can cheer for their favorite fighter, making the atmosphere lively and engaging.

3. Cultural Element:

In addition to the physical spectacle of the fights, there is often a cultural ritual involved in the show. The Wai Kru Ram Muay, a pre-fight dance, is a beautiful and deeply spiritual part of Muay Thai, where the fighters show respect to their teachers and ancestors before the match begins. The live music that accompanies the fight is also traditional and includes the pi java (a type of traditional Thai flute) and drums, which contribute to the atmosphere.

Where to Watch Muay Thai Shows in Chiang Mai

Siam Boxing Stadium: Located in the heart of Chiang Mai, this is one of the best places to watch live Muay Thai matches. They provide shows with exciting Muay Thai fights performed by professional fighters, usually in the evening.

Thapae Boxing Stadium: Another popular venue for watching Muay Thai in Chiang Mai, located near the Thapae Gate. This stadium hosts regular Muay Thai matches and shows, with both local fighters and tourists often participating in the action.

Muay Thai Live Shows: Some hotels and cultural centers also host Muay Thai live shows, where you can watch staged performances of this martial art in a more theatrical format. These shows often combine elements of both traditional dance and martial arts.

Tips for Enjoying Traditional Thai Dance and Muay Thai Shows

1. Be Respectful: Traditional Thai dance and Muay Thai are both deeply rooted in Thai culture. If you're attending a cultural show, it's important to be respectful of the performers and the rituals.

2. Arrive Early: For the best seats, especially at Khantoke dinner shows and Muay Thai matches, it's a good idea to arrive early to get a good view of the performance.

3. Dress Comfortably: While there are no strict dress codes, it's best to wear comfortable clothing if you're attending a show. For Muay Thai matches, consider wearing something casual, as it can get hot and energetic.

4. Participate in the Fun: Some Muay Thai shows and Thai dance performances encourage audience interaction. Whether you're invited to join a folk dance or get involved in a fun moment during a Muay Thai show, take the opportunity to participate and immerse yourself in the experience.

Learning Thai Cooking at Local Schools

Why Learn Thai Cooking in Chiang Mai?

1. Authentic Thai Cuisine: Chiang Mai is the heart of Northern Thai food. By learning to cook here, you can gain a deeper understanding of the region's unique flavors, ingredients, and cooking techniques.

2. Hands-on Experience: Many cooking schools provide immersive, hands-on cooking experiences where you not only learn how to make dishes but also get involved in every step of the process—from shopping for fresh ingredients at the local market to preparing and tasting the food.

3. Cultural Insight: Thai cooking classes are often intertwined with cultural stories, traditions, and local customs. It's an opportunity to learn about the history of dishes, their regional variations, and the importance of food in Thai society.

4. Take Home New Skills: The skills and recipes you learn can be taken back home to impress your family and friends with your newfound Thai culinary expertise.

What to Expect in a Thai Cooking Class in Chiang Mai

1. Market Tour:
Many cooking schools begin the class with a guided market tour, where you'll visit a local market to learn about the various fresh ingredients used in Thai cooking. You'll explore the vibrant stalls, taste local fruits and spices, and get to know the essential herbs and vegetables like lemongrass, galangal, kaffir lime, and Thai basil. This part of the class provides insight into the local food culture and how the ingredients are sourced.

2. Cooking Instruction:
After the market tour, you'll return to the school, where an experienced chef or instructor will guide you through the cooking process. Depending on the school, you may cook 5-7 dishes in a class. You'll learn how to make popular Thai dishes such as:

Pad Thai (stir-fried noodles)
Green Curry (a flavorful, aromatic curry with coconut milk)
Tom Yum Soup (spicy and sour soup with shrimp)

Som Tum (green papaya salad)
Sticky Rice with Mango (traditional dessert)
Khao Soi (Northern Thai coconut curry noodle soup)

You'll prepare each dish using authentic ingredients and follow traditional techniques that have been passed down through generations.

3. Cooking Stations:

Each student usually works at their own cooking station, equipped with all the tools needed to prepare the dishes. The classes are hands-on, so you'll have the opportunity to cook and chop the ingredients yourself, under the guidance of the chef. There's also plenty of time for tasting and adjusting flavors to your preference.

4. Enjoying the Meal:

At the end of the class, you'll sit down and enjoy the delicious dishes you've prepared. This is a great time to relax and reflect on what you've learned while savoring the fruits of your labor. Many schools even provide family-style dining, where everyone shares the dishes they've made.

5. Recipe Book or Certificate:

Most cooking schools provide participants with a recipe booklet containing all the dishes they learned during the class. Some schools may also give out a certificate of completion, which makes for a nice souvenir of your cooking experience.

Popular Cooking Schools in Chiang Mai

Here are some of the top-rated cooking schools in Chiang Mai:

1. Baipai Thai Cooking School

Overview: Located just outside the city center, Baipai is one of Chiang Mai's most famous cooking schools, extending a comprehensive cooking class experience. The school is known for its spacious, open-air kitchen and beautiful surroundings.
What to Expect: Classes typically begin with a visit to the market to gather ingredients. You'll learn to make 5-7 dishes and enjoy a wonderful, hands-on experience. The school

emphasizes Lanna-style cooking, a Northern Thai tradition.
Price Range: Around 1,500 – 2,000 THB per person.

2. Thai Farm Cooking School

Overview: Situated in the countryside, Thai Farm Cooking School provides a unique experience, focusing on organic ingredients grown on the farm. This school provides an immersive cooking experience in a natural, peaceful setting.
What to Expect: In addition to a market tour, you'll get a chance to pick some ingredients directly from the farm. Classes include a wide range of dishes and focus on using organic produce. The school provides different types of cooking classes, including half-day and full-day options.
Price Range: Around 1,200 – 2,500 THB per person.

3. Chiang Mai Thai Cookery School

Overview: This is one of the oldest and most established cooking schools in Chiang Mai. It is well-known for its professional instructors and fun, informative classes.

What to Expect: The school provides half-day and full-day classes, where students can learn to prepare a variety of dishes, ranging from soups and curries to appetizers and desserts. The emphasis is on authentic Thai cooking using local ingredients.
Price Range: Around 1,200 – 2,000 THB per person.

4. A Lot of Thai Cooking School

Overview: This cooking school provides a personalized cooking experience with small group sizes. It is highly rated for its friendly instructors and delicious recipes.
What to Expect: A market tour, followed by cooking a variety of Thai dishes such as green curry and Pad Thai. This school provides a relaxed environment where participants can learn at their own pace.
Price Range: Around 1,000 – 1,500 THB per person.

5. Smart Thai Cooking School

Overview: Located in the city center, Smart Thai Cooking School provides classes in both traditional Thai and vegetarian cooking. It is a popular choice for foodies who are looking for a more intimate and personalized experience.

What to Expect: Classes include visits to the local markets and cooking in a well-equipped kitchen. The school also provides vegetarian options for those who prefer plant-based dishes.

Price Range: Around 1,000 – 1,500 THB per person.

Tips for Choosing a Cooking School in Chiang Mai

1. Check Reviews: Make sure to read reviews online to find a school that has a good reputation for quality instruction and authentic experiences.

2. Consider Your Interests: If you're particularly interested in vegetarian cooking, look for schools that specialize in plant-based dishes. Some schools also provide specialized classes on street food or desserts.

3. Book in Advance: Cooking classes can fill up quickly, especially during peak tourist seasons, so it's a good idea to book your spot in advance.

4. Bring a Notepad: While most schools provide recipe booklets, it's always helpful to bring a notebook to jot down extra tips or modifications to recipes.

EXPLORING NATURE AND OUTDOOR ACTIVITIES

Doi Inthanon National Park

Doi Inthanon National Park, located approximately 70 kilometers southwest of Chiang Mai, is one of Thailand's most famous and diverse natural destinations. Known for its cool climate, stunning mountain views, lush rainforests, and vibrant wildlife, the park is often referred to as the "Roof of Thailand" because it contains the highest peak in the country, Doi Inthanon, which reaches an altitude of 2,565 meters (8,415 feet).

What to Expect at Doi Inthanon National Park

Doi Inthanon is not just a single peak, but a protected area covering over 1,000 square kilometers of rugged terrain. Visitors can experience a wide variety of landscapes, from tropical rainforests and cloud forests to grasslands and mountain streams. The park provides several attractions and activities, making it a perfect day trip for nature lovers, hikers, and photographers.

1. Doi Inthanon Peak

The park's highlight is undoubtedly the Doi Inthanon Summit, which provides panoramic views of the surrounding mountains and valleys. On clear days, you can see all the way to Myanmar. The summit is often shrouded in mist and cool temperatures, even in the summer, extending a refreshing escape from the heat of Chiang Mai.

2. The King and Queen Pagodas

Near the summit, you'll find the Phra Mahathat Naphamethinidon and Phra Mahathat Naphaphonphumisiri pagodas, built to honor the King and Queen of Thailand. The pagodas are beautifully decorated and are surrounded by well-maintained gardens, extending both a cultural and scenic experience.

3. Nature Trails and Hikes

The park provides several trails of varying difficulty levels, including:

Kew Mae Pan Nature Trail: A 2.6-kilometer trail through cloud forests, providing spectacular views of the mountains, waterfalls, and valleys. It's one of the most popular hiking routes in the park, especially for birdwatching. Ang Ka Nature Trail: A shorter, 300-meter trail that takes you through the park's high-altitude forest, extending insight into the unique plants and animals that thrive in the cool climate. Sirithan Waterfall Trail: A short trail leading to the stunning Sirithan Waterfall, one of the park's most picturesque waterfalls.

4. Waterfalls

Doi Inthanon is home to several beautiful waterfalls, with many located near the main road. Some of the most famous include:

Sirithan Waterfall: A 40-meter waterfall, located in the northern part of the park.
Wachirathan Waterfall: A large, dramatic waterfall located at the base of the park, near the main entrance.
Mae Ya Waterfall: A beautiful multi-tiered waterfall, located in the southern part of the park.

5. Birdwatching

Doi Inthanon is renowned for its birdwatching opportunities, with over 380 bird species recorded in the park. This makes it a hotspot for bird enthusiasts. Some of the notable species include the blue-throated barbet, the Siamese fireback, and various species of pheasants.

6. Hill Tribe Villages

The park is home to several ethnic hill tribes, such as the Hmong, Karen, and Lisu people. Visiting the villages provides a cultural experience and a chance to interact with locals who have lived in the mountains for generations. Some villages sell traditional handicrafts, including handmade textiles and silver jewelry.

7. Royal Projects

The Royal Project initiatives at Doi Inthanon aim to improve the livelihoods of local farmers and promote sustainable farming practices. Visitors can see various agricultural projects, including the cultivation of flowers, herbs, and fruits. The Hmong Market near the summit sells fresh produce, local handicrafts, and souvenirs.

How to Get to Doi Inthanon National Park

Doi Inthanon is about a 1.5 to 2-hour drive from Chiang Mai. The park is accessible by car, private tours, or songthaews (shared taxis). Here's how to get there:

1. By Car: The easiest way is to rent a car and drive yourself. The roads are well-maintained, but they can be winding and steep.
2. By Tour: Many travel agencies in Chiang Mai provide guided tours that take you to Doi Inthanon, including transport, a guide, and a visit to the various attractions.
3. By Songthaew: You can also hire a songthaew (shared red taxi) from Chiang Mai, but be prepared to negotiate the price.
4. By Motorbike/Scooter: If you're comfortable driving a scooter, it's a great way to explore at your own pace, though the roads to the summit can be challenging for novice riders.

Entrance Fees

Entrance Fee: The entrance fee for foreign tourists is approximately 300 THB per person.
Vehicle Fee: For those traveling by car, the entrance fee for the vehicle is around 30-60 THB.

Tips for Visiting Doi Inthanon

1. Dress Warmly: Even though it can be hot in Chiang Mai, temperatures at the summit can be significantly cooler. Bring a light jacket or sweater, especially in the mornings and evenings.
2. Be Prepared for Hiking: Some trails, like the Kew Mae Pan Nature Trail, can be challenging, so make sure to wear comfortable shoes suitable for walking on uneven ground.
3. Bring a Camera: The views and landscapes at Doi Inthanon are stunning, so don't forget to bring your camera or smartphone to capture the beauty.
4. Pack Snacks and Water: While there are some food options around the park, it's always good to bring your own water and snacks for longer hikes.
5. Hire a Guide: If you're interested in learning more about the plants, animals, and cultural significance of the area, consider hiring a local guide to enhance your experience.

Elephant Sanctuaries

Chiang Mai is one of the most popular places in Thailand for visitors to learn about and interact with elephants in a responsible and ethical way. The region is home to several elephant sanctuaries, where tourists can experience these majestic creatures in a safe, respectful, and sustainable environment. These sanctuaries focus on providing a natural habitat for elephants that have been rescued from harmful situations, such as the logging or tourism industries, and provide educational experiences that promote conservation and animal welfare.

Why Visit an Elephant Sanctuary in Chiang Mai?

1. Ethical Experience: Many of Chiang Mai's sanctuaries focus on ethical treatment, extending a safe space for elephants to roam freely without being subjected to the harsh treatment that is common in some tourist attractions. They provide a chance to interact with elephants in a non-exploitative way.

2. Animal Welfare: Sanctuaries rescue elephants from abusive situations such as forced labor or performances, and their main goal is to provide them with a better quality of life in a natural environment.

3. Education and Conservation: Visiting a sanctuary is an opportunity to learn about the important role elephants play in Thai culture and ecology, and to support the conservation efforts aimed at protecting these endangered animals.

4. Unique Experience: Visitors have the chance to get up close to elephants in a more natural setting, without the stress of rides, shows, or tricks. Many sanctuaries provide activities like feeding, bathing, and walking with elephants, allowing guests to bond with these gentle creatures in a relaxed and safe environment.

Top Elephant Sanctuaries in Chiang Mai

1. Elephant Nature Park

Overview: Elephant Nature Park is one of the most famous ethical elephant sanctuaries in Chiang Mai. Founded by Lek Chailert, a well-known animal rights advocate, this sanctuary rescues elephants from exploitative industries like logging and tourism. The park is located about 60 km from Chiang Mai and is set in a peaceful valley.

What to Expect: Visitors can learn about the elephants' backgrounds, observe them in their natural habitat, and even help bathe and feed them. The sanctuary provides a safe, stress-free environment where the elephants can roam freely.

Key Activities: Elephant feeding, bathing, nature walks, and educational talks on elephant conservation.

Price Range: Around 1,500 – 2,500 THB per person for a day tour.

2. Elephant Jungle Sanctuary

Overview: Elephant Jungle Sanctuary is a family-run sanctuary that provides a safe haven for elephants rescued from the tourism and logging industries. The sanctuary is known for its ethical practices, and it focuses on creating a comfortable environment for the elephants to roam, interact, and live peacefully.

What to Expect: Visitors get to learn about the elephants' histories, bathe them in the river, and help feed them. The sanctuary also provides an educational experience on the challenges facing elephants in Thailand.

Key Activities: Bathing the elephants, feeding them, trekking through the jungle, and learning about their rescue stories.

Price Range: Around 1,500 – 3,000 THB per person, depending on the package.

3. Elephant PooPooPaper Park

Overview: While not a traditional elephant sanctuary, Elephant PooPooPaper Park provides a unique experience where visitors can learn about how elephant dung is used to make paper. The park educates visitors on sustainable practices and supports elephant conservation.

What to Expect: Tourists can explore how the park processes elephant dung into eco-friendly paper, and learn about the elephants that provide the raw material. It's a more hands-on and quirky way to support conservation while educating the public.

Key Activities: Watching the process of making paper from elephant dung, creating your own paper products, and interacting with elephants in a responsible way.

Price Range: Around 200 – 500 THB per person.

4. Patara Elephant Farm

Overview: Patara Elephant Farm is another well-respected sanctuary that focuses on the well-being of its elephants. The farm's goal is to create a sustainable environment where elephants are cared for and can live naturally. Visitors can have an intimate experience by taking on the role of a "Mahout" (elephant caretaker).

What to Expect: This sanctuary provides an immersive experience where you can feed, bathe, and ride elephants. The farm prides itself on allowing tourists to interact with elephants in a non-exploitative manner while educating them on elephant care and conservation.

Key Activities: Becoming a "Mahout" for the day, feeding and bathing elephants, and learning about their individual stories.

Price Range: Around 2,500 – 4,000 THB per person.

5. Chiang Mai Elephant Sanctuary

Overview: Chiang Mai Elephant Sanctuary is a more recently established sanctuary that focuses on rescuing elephants from exploitative situations and providing them with a more humane lifestyle. The sanctuary is situated outside the city, surrounded by lush jungle, extending a peaceful setting for elephants to thrive.

What to Expect: Visitors can enjoy intimate experiences such as walking with elephants, feeding them, and bathing them in natural streams. The sanctuary also provides an educational aspect, focusing on the history of elephants in Thailand.

Key Activities: Feeding elephants, walking with them in the jungle, and learning about their history and conservation.

Price Range: Around 1,500 – 2,500 THB per person.

What to Expect at Elephant Sanctuaries

No Riding: Most ethical sanctuaries have stopped the practice of elephant riding. Riding elephants, often associated with cruel training methods, is no longer allowed at these places.

Feeding and Bathing: Guests often participate in activities such as feeding elephants fruits like bananas or watermelon, and bathing them in a river or mud pit, which is both a fun and meaningful way to care for the elephants.

Learning About Elephant Welfare: Many sanctuaries have education centers or provide talks where visitors learn about the history and issues surrounding elephants, including the threats they face in the wild, the importance of their conservation, and the ethical practices the sanctuaries follow.

Elephant Enrichment: In addition to regular meals, sanctuaries often provide enrichment activities for elephants to stimulate their mental and physical well-being, such as puzzle feeders, social interaction with other elephants, and access to large open areas.

Tips for Visiting Elephant Sanctuaries

1. Choose Ethical Sanctuaries: Avoid places that provide elephant rides, shows, or any form of elephant performance. Ethical sanctuaries prioritize the well-being of the animals and provide educational, hands-on experiences instead.

2. Wear Comfortable Clothing: Since you'll likely be walking, feeding, and bathing elephants, wear comfortable clothing that you don't mind getting dirty, especially if you're interacting with elephants in the water or mud.

3. Respect the Elephants: Always follow the rules set by the sanctuary and maintain a respectful distance from the elephants. Although the elephants are well-treated, it's important to understand their space and not cause them stress.

4. Support Ethical Practices: Your visit helps fund the rescue efforts and conservation projects of these sanctuaries. Consider donating or purchasing souvenirs that support elephant welfare.

Zip Lining and Jungle Adventures

Zip Lining

Zip lining provides the chance to soar above the jungle treetops, enjoying stunning aerial views of the forest below. Chiang Mai is home to several world-class zip line operators, and most zip line tours are eco-friendly, with a strong emphasis on safety and conservation.

Popular Zip Lining Operators in Chiang Mai

1. Flight of the Gibbon

Overview: One of the most popular and established zip lining experiences in Chiang Mai, Flight of the Gibbon provides a multi-cable zip line course through the rainforest canopy. The company is known for its eco-friendly approach and the conservation efforts to protect wildlife and the environment. What to Expect: Tourists can experience a variety of activities, including zip lining through the treetops, canopy bridges, and even hiking in the surrounding forest. The tour lasts around 3-4 hours and includes a safety briefing before you begin.

Price Range: Approximately 2,000 – 3,000 THB per person, depending on the package and season.

2. Chiang Mai Jungle Flight

Overview: extending one of the longest and most thrilling zip line courses in Thailand, Chiang Mai Jungle Flight takes you through dense jungles and past waterfalls, providing an adrenaline-packed experience with a focus on safety and environmental conservation.

What to Expect: This zip line adventure provides multiple routes, including sky bridges and abseiling (rappelling), making it a more interactive and action-packed experience. The tour includes stops for birdwatching and exploration of the lush greenery.

Price Range: Around 1,500 – 3,500 THB per person, depending on the course and time of year.

3. The Zipline Chiang Mai

Overview: The Zipline Chiang Mai provides a shorter, but equally exciting zip lining experience, with a focus on safety and fun. This is a great option for those who want a quick adventure without committing to a full-day tour.

What to Expect: The tour includes several zip lines and canopy walks, all while providing aerial views of the surrounding mountains and forest. It's a thrilling yet accessible option for first-time zip liners.

Price Range: Around 1,500 – 2,500 THB per person.

Other Jungle Adventures

1. Jungle Trekking

Overview: Trekking through the rainforests of Chiang Mai provides an unparalleled opportunity to explore the wild beauty of northern Thailand. Tours range from easy half-day treks to challenging multi-day hikes, where you can explore dense jungles, encounter wildlife, and visit remote hill tribe villages.

Popular Routes: Some of the most popular trekking routes include the Doi Inthanon National Park, Mae Taeng, and the Chiang Dao area, which provide beautiful trekking trails through lush greenery, mountains, and valleys.

Price Range: Half-day treks can range from 500 – 1,000 THB, while more extensive multi-day treks can cost between 2,000 –5,000 THB, depending on the length of the trek and the included services.

2. ATV Adventures

Overview: For those who prefer a faster-paced adventure, ATV (All-Terrain Vehicle) tours provide a thrilling way to explore Chiang Mai's jungles and rural areas. These tours take you on off-road tracks, through muddy trails, and past waterfalls, making for an exciting and unique experience.

What to Expect: The tours range from beginner-friendly rides to more challenging adventures. Some ATV tours also include a stop at an elephant sanctuary or a local village for a cultural experience.

Price Range: Around 1,500 – 3,000 THB for a half-day ATV adventure.

3. White Water Rafting

Overview: If you're looking for a water-based adventure, Chiang Mai's Mae Taeng River provides some of the best white-water rafting experiences in Thailand. Rafting through the mountain rivers and gorges is a thrilling way to experience the region's stunning landscapes.

What to Expect: You'll navigate fast-moving rapids, while surrounded by lush jungle and dramatic cliffs. Most tours provide a safety briefing and experienced guides to ensure a safe experience.
Price Range: Half-day rafting tours typically cost between 1,500 – 2,500 THB.

4. Jungle Safari Tours

Overview: For a more relaxed but still adventurous experience, consider going on a jungle safari tour, which combines elements of nature walks, wildlife spotting, and visiting remote villages. Some tours also provide opportunities for swimming in waterfalls and sightseeing.
What to Expect: These tours often include a guide who will point out local flora and fauna, providing educational insights into the ecosystems of the jungle. It's a great way to experience the natural beauty of Chiang Mai without the intensity of zip lining or white-water rafting.
Price Range: Around 1,000 – 2,500 THB per person, depending on the duration and inclusions.

5. Night Jungle Trekking

Overview: For something different, try a night jungle trek, where you explore the rainforest after dark. This adventure lets you discover the nocturnal creatures of the jungle, such as fireflies, night birds, and insects. What to Expect: With a local guide, you'll explore the jungle under the stars, learning about the ecosystem and wildlife that only comes to life at night. It's a unique way to connect with nature. Price Range: Around 1,000 – 2,000 THB per person.

Safety and Tips for Jungle Adventures

1. Safety Gear: For zip lining, ATV riding, or rafting, ensure that the company provides appropriate safety gear such as helmets, harnesses, life jackets, and first aid kits.
2. Physical Fitness: Many jungle activities, especially trekking, can be physically demanding. Make sure you're in good physical condition, and choose the difficulty level that matches your fitness level.
3. Guides: Always go with a certified guide who is experienced in the activity and familiar with

the local terrain. This ensures safety and a better experience, as the guide can share interesting insights about the area.

4. Respect Nature: Be mindful of your surroundings, especially in nature reserves and wildlife areas. Avoid disturbing wildlife and stay on designated paths.

5. Hydrate and Protect: Bring plenty of water, wear sunscreen, and wear light, breathable clothing to protect yourself from the sun and insects. In the jungle, mosquito repellent is highly recommended.

Trekking and Waterfall Hikes

Popular Trekking Routes in Chiang Mai

1. Doi Inthanon National Park

Overview: As the highest peak in Thailand at 2,565 meters, Doi Inthanon provides a wide variety of treks, from short walks to challenging multi-day hikes. The park is known for its cool climate, rich biodiversity, and impressive waterfalls. It is home to a number of hill tribes and provides some of the most stunning views in the region.

Popular Trails:

Kew Mae Pan Nature Trail: A moderate 3.2 km trek through cloud forests, extending spectacular views of the surrounding mountains and valleys. It's one of the most popular trails for visitors and takes about 2-3 hours to complete.

Ang Ka Nature Trail: A short, easy trail that takes you through temperate forests and provides an opportunity to explore the unique ecosystems of the park.

Waterfalls: Doi Inthanon is home to several stunning waterfalls, including Wachirathan Waterfall and Sirithan Waterfall. These waterfalls can be accessed via short walks from the main road.

Price Range: Entry fees to Doi Inthanon National Park are typically around 100-200 THB for foreigners. Guided trekking tours can range from 1,500 – 3,000 THB per day.

2. Mae Taeng and Elephant Nature Park

Overview: Located around 60 km north of Chiang Mai, the Mae Taeng area provides lush jungles, rolling hills, and several waterfalls. The Elephant Nature Park is also located here, providing opportunities to combine trekking with a visit to this renowned sanctuary.

Popular Trails:

Mae Taeng Waterfall Trek: This 2-3 hour hike takes you through lush jungles and past waterfalls, extending a peaceful and immersive experience in nature.

Elephant Sanctuary Trek: Many tours in this area combine trekking with visits to elephant sanctuaries. It's a great way to learn about conservation efforts while exploring the forests and waterfalls.

Price Range: Day treks in Mae Taeng can range from 1,200 – 2,500 THB, including transportation and a guide.

3. Chiang Dao

Overview: The Chiang Dao region, located about 70 km north of Chiang Mai, is known for its rugged mountains, deep caves, and waterfalls. It provides some of the most remote and peaceful treks in Chiang Mai, with fewer crowds compared to other areas.

Popular Trails:

Chiang Dao Waterfall Trek: This hike takes you through beautiful jungles and past waterfalls to Chiang Dao Cave, one of the longest caves in Thailand. The trek is moderate in difficulty and typically lasts 4-5 hours.

Doi Chiang Dao Trek: This trek leads to the summit of Doi Chiang Dao, the third-highest mountain in Thailand. It's a challenging multi-day hike that rewards trekkers with incredible panoramic views and encounters with hill tribes.

Price Range: Chiang Dao treks typically cost around 1,500 – 3,000 THB for a day trip. Multi-day treks can range from 3,500 – 6,000 THB.

4. Huay Tung Tao Lake to Mae Sa Waterfall

Overview: This easy-to-moderate trek takes you through scenic forests, past local villages, and leads to Mae Sa Waterfall, one of the most famous in the area. It's a perfect option for those looking for a shorter trek with a rewarding waterfall at the end.

What to Expect: The trail is about 6 km long and can be completed in about 3-4 hours. The hike is fairly straightforward, with gentle slopes, making it suitable for beginners or those with limited trekking experience.

Price Range: Guided treks for this trail usually cost between 600 – 1,500 THB per person.

5. The Monk's Trail

Overview: The Monk's Trail is a popular and moderate trek that leads from Wat Phra That Doi Suthep to the summit of Doi Suthep. It's a beautiful hike that takes you through lush forests and provides stunning views of Chiang Mai.

What to Expect: The trail is about 3.5 km long, and it takes around 2-3 hours to complete. It's a peaceful and scenic route, with many trekkers enjoying the journey for both its natural beauty and spiritual significance.

Price Range: Most visitors do the Monk's Trail independently. If hiring a guide, the cost typically ranges from 500 – 1,000 THB.

Waterfall Hikes in Chiang Mai

1. Mae Sa Waterfall

Overview: Located about 20 km from Chiang Mai, Mae Sa Waterfall is a series of 10 waterfalls cascading down the hillside. The trail to the waterfall is well-maintained, making it a popular destination for both trekkers and families.

What to Expect: The trek is easy, and visitors can enjoy the beauty of the forest, walk up to the various levels of waterfalls, and swim in the natural pools.

Price Range: Entry fees are typically 20 – 50 THB.

2. Huay Kaew Waterfall

Overview: Situated near Doi Suthep, this waterfall is one of the easiest to reach from Chiang Mai. The trail to the waterfall is short but provides a great opportunity to experience the jungle environment and listen to the sounds of the cascading water.

What to Expect: A short 30-minute hike leads to the waterfall, which is a popular spot for locals and tourists alike.

Price Range: Free entry.

3. Wachirathan Waterfall

Overview: Located in Doi Inthanon National Park, Wachirathan Waterfall is one of the largest and most impressive waterfalls in the region. The waterfall is easily accessible by car and provides an awe-inspiring view as it cascades down the cliffs.

What to Expect: While the main waterfall can be accessed easily from the parking area, you can also take a short walk along the path to see the falls from different angles.

Price Range: Entry fees to Doi Inthanon National Park apply.

4. Sirithan Waterfall

Overview: Another stunning waterfall located in Doi Inthanon National Park, Sirithan Waterfall is a beautiful spot to visit while trekking through the park. It's known for its picturesque setting and refreshing atmosphere.

What to Expect: A short walk of about 15 minutes leads to the falls, and visitors can enjoy the serene surroundings and cool mist from the waterfall.

Price Range: Entry fees to Doi Inthanon National Park apply.

Tips for Trekking and Waterfall Hikes

1. Wear Proper Footwear: Trekking boots or sturdy hiking shoes are essential, especially if

you're trekking to waterfalls or through wet areas.

2. Bring Water: It's important to stay hydrated, so always carry a water bottle, especially for longer hikes.

3. Insect Repellent: The jungle can be full of mosquitoes and other insects, so don't forget to apply insect repellent before heading out.

4. Local Guides: For more remote hikes, hiring a local guide is recommended to ensure safety and to enrich your experience with knowledge of the area's culture and wildlife.

5. Pack Light: Keep your pack light and only bring the essentials—water, snacks, sunscreen, and a camera to capture the beautiful views.

The Mae Ping River Cruise Experience

The Mae Ping River is one of the major rivers in northern Thailand, flowing for over 1,200 kilometers. It runs through Chiang Mai, cutting across lush green landscapes and charming rural communities. The river has historically been vital for local transportation, farming, and trade, with many small villages nestled along its banks. Today, the river serves as an important source of natural beauty, and its peaceful waters make it an ideal location for cruises and boat tours.

Types of Mae Ping River Cruises

1. Traditional Boat Cruises

Description: These cruises typically use long-tail boats or traditional wooden boats, extending an intimate experience as you glide along the river. Many of these boats are designed to accommodate small groups, making them perfect for couples or families.

What to Expect: During these cruises, you'll enjoy the gentle motion of the boat while taking in the view of the lush riverside vegetation, local farms, and rural villages. You may also pass temples, such as Wat Chai Mongkhon and Wat Tha Phae, which are beautifully situated along the river.

Duration: Cruises can last from 1 to 2 hours, but some private tours can extend longer depending on the itinerary.

2. Luxury Dinner Cruises

Description: For those seeking a more luxurious experience, dinner cruises on the Mae Ping River provide a romantic and elegant way to enjoy Chiang Mai's beauty. These cruises typically feature buffet-style meals with both Thai and international cuisine.

What to Expect: As you dine, you'll enjoy stunning views of the sunset over the river and nearby mountains. The riverbanks are lit up with lights from local restaurants, creating a warm and peaceful atmosphere as you relax and enjoy your meal.

Duration: These cruises often last about 2-3 hours, starting in the early evening and ending after dark.

3. Cultural and Historical Cruises

Description: These cruises focus on the cultural and historical significance of the river and its surrounding areas. Local guides share the history of the river and the communities that live along it. You may also visit traditional homes, markets, and local temples during the cruise.

What to Expect: In addition to the river views, this type of cruise provides an educational experience where you'll learn about the lifestyle of people living along the Mae Ping River, their farming techniques, and the river's role in their daily lives.

Duration: Cultural cruises can range from 2 to 4 hours, depending on the stops included in the tour.

Price Range for Mae Ping River Cruises

The cost of a Mae Ping River cruise can vary depending on the type of tour you choose and the services provide ed:

1. Traditional Boat Cruises:

Price Range: 300 – 800 THB per person.
Private boat tours can cost around 1,500 – 3,500 THB, depending on the duration and inclusions.

2. Luxury Dinner Cruises:

Price Range: 800 – 1,500 THB per person, depending on the type of meal and the boat.

3. Cultural and Historical Cruises:

Price Range: 500 – 1,500 THB per person.
Guided tours with cultural stops may cost between 1,000 – 2,000 THB per person.

Best Time for a Mae Ping River Cruise

The best time to take a river cruise is in the cool season (from November to February) when the weather is pleasant, and the river's surroundings are lush and green. Early morning cruises are perfect for those who want to experience the peaceful serenity of the river and enjoy the morning mist. Sunset cruises provide a romantic atmosphere as you can witness the sunset over the mountains and the river.

Things to Bring on a Mae Ping River Cruise

1. Sunscreen: Protect your skin from the sun, especially during midday cruises.
2. Camera: The scenic views are perfect for photos, so don't forget your camera or smartphone.
3. Hat and Sunglasses: Essential for protecting yourself from the sun during outdoor cruises.
4. Water: Stay hydrated, especially if you're doing a longer tour.

5. Light Jacket: If you're going on an evening or sunset cruise, bring a light jacket as it can get cooler as the sun sets.

CULINARY DELIGHTS

Must-Try Dishes

1. Khao Soi (Northern Thai Curry Noodles)

Description: Khao Soi is Chiang Mai's signature dish, a delicious curry noodle soup that combines rich, coconut-based broth with crispy fried noodles on top. It's typically served with either chicken or beef, and you can garnish it with pickled mustard greens, lime, and chili paste for extra flavor.

Price Range:
Street Food: 50 – 80 THB
Restaurants: 100 – 150 THB

2. Sai Oua (Northern Thai Sausage)

Description: This aromatic and flavorful sausage is made from pork mixed with herbs, including lemongrass, kaffir lime leaves, and garlic. It's grilled to perfection and served as a snack or appetizer.

Price Range:
Street Food: 50 – 80 THB
Restaurants: 100 – 150 THB

3. Gaeng Hang Lay (Pork Curry)

Description: This is a unique Northern Thai curry made with tender pieces of pork slow-cooked in a rich, mildly spicy broth flavored with ginger, garlic, turmeric, and tamarind. The curry has a savory-sweet flavor that's distinct from other Thai curries.

Price Range:
Street Food: 60 – 100 THB
Restaurants: 120 – 200 THB

4. Nam Prik Ong (Northern Thai Chili Dip)

Description: Nam Prik Ong is a flavorful chili dip made with ground pork, tomatoes, and various spices. It's typically served with vegetables, herbs, and sticky rice for dipping. It's a tangy and mildly spicy dish, perfect for sharing.

Price Range:
Street Food: 40 – 60 THB
Restaurants: 80 – 120 THB

5. Khao Niew Mamuang (Sticky Rice with Mango)

Description: A sweet and iconic Thai dessert made of sticky rice served with fresh mango and drizzled with coconut milk. It's a refreshing and satisfying dessert, perfect after a spicy meal.

Price Range:
Street Food: 40 – 60 THB
Restaurants: 60 – 100 THB

6. Laab (Spicy Minced Meat Salad)

Description: Laab is a popular dish in northern Thailand, consisting of minced pork, chicken, or beef, mixed with fresh herbs, lime, and chili, and served with sticky rice. It's a tangy and spicy dish, packed with flavor.

Price Range:
Street Food: 50 – 80 THB
Restaurants: 100 – 150 THB

7. Som Tum (Green Papaya Salad)

Description: While Som Tum is more commonly associated with Isan (northeastern Thailand), it's widely available in Chiang Mai as well. This dish consists of shredded green papaya, chili, fish sauce, lime, and peanuts, creating a sweet, sour, spicy, and salty flavor profile.

Price Range:
Street Food: 40 – 60 THB
Restaurants: 80 – 120 THB

8. Sundried Pork (Moo Dad Deaw)

Description: A beloved snack in northern Thailand, Moo Dad Deaw is strips of pork marinated in soy sauce, sugar, and garlic, then dried in the sun and deep-fried until crispy. It's typically served with a side of sticky rice and dipping sauce.

Price Range:
Street Food: 50 – 80 THB
Restaurants: 100 – 150 THB

9. Khao Ka Moo (Stewed Pork Leg)

Description: This dish features a braised pork leg served with rice, topped with a rich, savory sauce. It's a hearty and satisfying meal, with the tender pork falling apart in your mouth.

Price Range:
Street Food: 50 – 80 THB
Restaurants: 100 – 150 THB

10. Sticky Rice with Fried Chicken (Khao Niew Gai Tod)

Description: A classic combination of crispy fried chicken paired with sticky rice. The chicken is marinated in herbs and spices, giving it a fragrant and flavorful taste.

Price Range:
Street Food: 60 – 100 THB
Restaurants: 100 – 150 THB

11. Gaeng Kiew Wan (Green Curry)

Description: While not exclusive to Chiang Mai, the green curry is a staple of Thai cuisine. Made with coconut milk, green curry paste, basil, and eggplant, this dish is aromatic and rich, often paired with chicken, beef, or tofu.

Price Range:
Street Food: 60 – 100 THB
Restaurants: 120 – 180 THB

12. Fried Fish with Spicy Tamarind Sauce

Description: This dish features deep-fried fish, usually tilapia, served with a tangy and spicy tamarind sauce. The combination of crispy fish and zesty sauce makes for a delicious and satisfying meal.

Price Range:
Street Food: 100 – 150 THB
Restaurants: 150 – 250 THB

Street Food Markets in Chiang Mai and Where to Find Them

1. Chiang Mai Sunday Walking Street (Tha Pae Walking Street)

Location: Ratchadamnoen Road, Old City (near Tha Pae Gate)
Time: Every Sunday from 4:00 PM to 10:00 PM
Overview: The Sunday Walking Street is one of the most popular street markets in Chiang Mai. It spans Ratchadamnoen Road in the Old City, extending a huge selection of street food, local snacks, and delicacies. You'll find dishes like Khao Soi, Sai Oua (Northern Thai sausage), grilled meats, sticky rice with mango, and more.

What to Try:

Khao Soi
Grilled Meat Skewers
Fried Banana Fritters
Sticky Rice with Mango (Khao Niew Mamuang)

2. Chiang Mai Night Bazaar

Location: Chang Klan Road, near the eastern side of the Old City
Time: Every day from 6:00 PM to 12:00 AM
Overview: The Night Bazaar is a must-visit market in Chiang Mai, extending an eclectic mix of local handicrafts, souvenirs, and, of course, street food. It's one of the best places to try a variety of Thai dishes in one place, from Thai-style grilled chicken to pork skewers and fried noodles.

What to Try:

Khao Ka Moo (Stewed Pork Leg)
Fried Fish with Tamarind Sauce
Pad Thai
Fried Spring Rolls

3. Warorot Market (Kad Luang)

Location: Chinatown, Warorot Road, near the Ping River
Time: Every day from 6:00 AM to 8:00 PM
Overview: Warorot Market is one of Chiang Mai's oldest and most famous markets, known for its fresh produce, clothing, and street food. The market is an excellent spot to sample local

Northern Thai dishes and try ingredients used in traditional cooking. It's a great market to explore during the day, but the food stalls become even more vibrant in the evenings.

What to Try:

Nam Prik Ong (Chili Dip)
Khao Niew Gai Tod (Sticky Rice with Fried Chicken)
Fried Insects
Sticky Rice Cakes

4. Chang Phuak Gate Night Market

Location: Chang Phuak Gate, North of the Old City
Time: Every day from 5:00 PM to 11:00 PM
Overview: Famous for the iconic "Cowboy Hat Lady", who serves delicious grilled meats and pork skewers, this market is a favorite among both locals and tourists. The market is smaller compared to the Night Bazaar, but it's packed with tasty local food.

What to Try:

Grilled Pork Skewers (Moo Ping)
Sticky Rice with Mango

Pad See Ew (Stir-fried Noodles)
Sundried Pork (Moo Dad Deaw)

5. Nimmanhaemin Night Market

Location: Nimmanhaemin Road, west of the Old City
Time: Every day from 6:00 PM to 10:00 PM
Overview: Nimmanhaemin is a trendy area in Chiang Mai, and its night market provides a more modern street food experience. Expect a mix of traditional Thai food and international options, all served in a more fashionable setting. The market is especially popular among locals and younger tourists.

What to Try:

Sushi Rolls
Thai Crepes
Fried Chicken
Burgers and Sandwiches

6. Sunday Market at the Three Kings Monument

Location: Three Kings Monument, near the Old City
Time: Every Sunday, from 10:00 AM to 4:00 PM (earlier than the Sunday Walking Street)
Overview: This smaller Sunday market is perfect for exploring while enjoying the local street food scene. It's located near the Three Kings Monument, a historical site in Chiang Mai. You'll find a mix of artisan goods, handmade crafts, and plenty of food stalls extending authentic dishes.

What to Try:

Khao Soi
Mango Sticky Rice
Grilled Sausages
Noodles and Dumplings

7. Sompet Market

Location: Near Thapae Road (close to the Old City)
Time: Every day from 7:00 AM to 8:00 PM
Overview: Sompet Market is a popular local market known for its diverse extending s,

including both fresh produce and street food. The market has a local charm, and it's one of the best places to enjoy Chiang Mai's authentic street food without the large crowds.

What to Try:

Pork Skewers (Moo Ping)
Coconut Ice Cream
Fried Fish Cakes
Sweet and Salty Thai Crepes

8. Mueang Mai Market

Location: Near the Ping River, close to the Warorot Market
Time: Every day from 6:00 AM to 8:00 PM
Overview: Mueang Mai Market is a bustling market that provides both fresh ingredients and street food. It's a local favorite for affordable meals, and you can find everything from traditional Thai rice noodles to grilled skewers and spicy curries.

What to Try:

Khao Kha Moo (Stewed Pork Leg)
Pad Thai
Curry Noodles

Fried Spring Rolls

9. Saturday Night Market (Wua Lai Walking Street)

Location: Wua Lai Road, South of the Old City (near the Chiang Mai Gate)
Time: Every Saturday from 4:00 PM to 10:00 PM
Overview: Similar to the Sunday Walking Street, the Saturday Night Market in Chiang Mai is a bustling event that runs along Wua Lai Road. The market is famous for extending a mix of local street food, crafts, and art. The relaxed atmosphere makes it a great place to spend an evening exploring Chiang Mai's food culture.

What to Try:

Khao Soi
Sticky Rice with Mango
Fried Tofu
Sundried Pork

Best Restaurants and Hidden Eateries

1. Khao Soi Khun Yai

Cuisine: Northern Thai (Specialty: Khao Soi)
Location: Nimmanhaemin Road, Soi 17
Overview: Khao Soi Khun Yai is a beloved spot known for its authentic Khao Soi (Northern Thai curry noodles). The restaurant is tucked away in a quiet part of the Nimmanhaemin area and is famous for its rich broth, tender chicken, and crispy noodles. A must-visit for anyone craving the iconic dish.
What to Try: Khao Soi, Sai Oua (Northern Thai sausage)
Price Range: 50 – 100 THB

2. The River Market

Cuisine: Thai (Specialty: Seafood and Thai Fusion)
Location: 8 Charoenrat Road, Riverside
Overview: Situated on the banks of the Ping River, The River Market provides an elegant atmosphere with beautiful views of the water. The restaurant focuses on fresh seafood and authentic Thai flavors, making it a great spot for a relaxed meal by the river.

What to Try: Grilled Fish, Green Curry with Shrimp, Sticky Rice with Mango
Price Range: 200 – 500 THB

3. Huen Phen

Cuisine: Northern Thai
Location: 112 Ratchamanka Road, Old City
Overview: Huen Phen is a local institution serving authentic Northern Thai cuisine in a charming traditional setting. The restaurant has been a favorite for years, extending dishes like Gaeng Hang Lay (pork curry), Khao Niew Moo Ping (sticky rice with grilled pork), and Nam Prik Ong (spicy chili dip).
What to Try: Gaeng Hang Lay, Khao Niew Moo Ping, Nam Prik Ong
Price Range: 100 – 200 THB

4. Dash! Teak House

Cuisine: Thai (Specialty: Northern Thai Dishes)
Location: 38/2-3 Moon Muang Road, Old City
Overview: Dash! Teak House is a beautifully restored teakwood house, serving both traditional and contemporary Northern Thai dishes. The restaurant provides a cozy and intimate dining experience with an extensive

menu of Thai classics, alongside signature drinks.
What to Try: Khao Soi, Northern Thai Sausage, Fried Tofu
Price Range: 150 – 300 THB

5. Café de Chiang Mai

Cuisine: Fusion Thai and International
Location: Near Nimmanhaemin Road
Overview: Café de Chiang Mai is a fusion café that blends international influences with traditional Thai ingredients. The modern and cozy atmosphere is perfect for breakfast or brunch. Their smoothies, Thai-inspired salads, and pasta are especially popular.
What to Try: Mango Sticky Rice Pancakes, Pad Thai, Thai Iced Tea
Price Range: 100 – 200 THB

6. The Larder

Cuisine: International (Specialty: European and Mediterranean)
Location: Soi 1, Nimmanhaemin Road
Overview: The Larder is a chic, European-style bistro extending a menu inspired by Mediterranean flavors. It's known for its steaks, sauces, and fresh salads. It's a great

place to enjoy something outside the traditional Thai fare and savor a high-quality, fine dining experience.

What to Try: Rib-eye Steak, Seafood Linguine, Apple Pie

Price Range: 300 – 600 THB

7. Kanjana

Cuisine: Thai (Specialty: Northern Thai Dishes)

Location: Siri Mangkalajarn Road, near Nimmanhaemin

Overview: Kanjana is an authentic, family-owned Thai restaurant in Chiang Mai that provides a wide variety of Northern Thai dishes. It's known for its excellent service and authentic flavors, making it a favorite among locals and tourists alike.

What to Try: Gaeng Hang Lay, Khao Niew Moo Ping, Pad Ka Prao

Price Range: 100 – 250 THB

8. Riverside Bar & Restaurant

Cuisine: Thai and International

Location: 9-13 Charoenrat Road, Riverside

Overview: Riverside Bar & Restaurant is a relaxed, riverside dining spot with a lively atmosphere. They serve both Thai and

international dishes, extending great options for dinner while enjoying the scenic view of the Ping River.
What to Try: Crispy Fish, Massaman Curry, Papaya Salad
Price Range: 150 – 400 THB

9. Laab Ubon

Cuisine: Isan (Northeastern Thai)
Location: Nimmanhaemin Road, near the mall
Overview: Laab Ubon specializes in the flavors of Isan (Northeastern Thailand), extending spicy dishes like Laab (spicy minced meat salad) and Som Tum (green papaya salad). The rustic setting and casual atmosphere make it a favorite for those who love spicy and bold flavors.
What to Try: Laab Moo, Som Tum, Sticky Rice
Price Range: 50 – 150 THB

10. Ginger & Kafe

Cuisine: Thai and International Fusion
Location: 13-15 Thapae Road, Old City
Overview: Ginger & Kafe is a stylish fusion restaurant extending a variety of traditional Thai dishes with a modern twist. The restaurant's unique interior and cozy ambiance

make it perfect for a special evening. They also provide a high tea experience, which is quite popular among visitors.
What to Try: Spicy Thai Curry, Tom Yum Soup, Western-Style Desserts
Price Range: 150 – 300 THB

11. Anchan Vegetarian Restaurant

Cuisine: Vegetarian and Vegan Thai
Location: 16/3 Soi 7, Moonmuang Road, Old City
Overview: Anchan is a hidden gem for those seeking healthy, vegetarian, and vegan Thai food. The restaurant provides flavorful dishes using organic ingredients, and it's known for its creative take on traditional Thai dishes.
What to Try: Vegan Khao Soi, Thai Green Curry, Mango Sticky Rice
Price Range: 100 – 200 THB

12. The Good View Village

Cuisine: Thai, International
Location: Thapoa Road, Riverside
Overview: Located along the river, The Good View Village provides a relaxed atmosphere and scenic views, perfect for enjoying a meal in the evening. The menu provides a range of

local and international dishes, from traditional Thai favorites to Western-style meals.

What to Try: Grilled Seafood, Tom Yum Goong, Beef Tenderloin

Price Range: 150 – 350 THB

13. Coco's Café

Cuisine: International (Specialty: Breakfast and Brunch)

Location: Nimmanhaemin Road

Overview: A great place to grab a coffee and enjoy a hearty breakfast or brunch. Coco's Café serves a variety of Western and Thai-inspired breakfast dishes, including smoothie bowls, avocado toast, and pancakes.

What to Try: Smoothie Bowls, Avocado Toast, Eggs Benedict

Price Range: 100 – 200 THB

Cooking Classes and Local Food Tours

1. Baipai Thai Cooking School

Cuisine: Thai (Specialty: Authentic Thai Dishes)
Location: Sankampaeng Road, East of the Old City
Overview: Baipai Thai Cooking School is one of the most famous cooking schools in Chiang Mai. Located in a beautiful setting, this school provides an immersive experience into traditional Thai cooking. Classes are hands-on, and you'll learn how to prepare a variety of dishes, from curries to stir-fries.
What to Expect: A visit to the local market, hands-on cooking session, and a delicious meal of your creations.
Class Price Range: 1,200 – 2,500 THB per person (depending on the class)
Booking: Pre-booking required

2. Thai Farm Cooking School

Cuisine: Thai (Specialty: Organic and Farm-to-Table)
Location: Sankampaeng, Chiang Mai (about 30 minutes from the city center)

Overview: Located in the scenic countryside, Thai Farm Cooking School takes you on a journey from the farm to the kitchen. The classes are taught in a beautiful garden surrounded by fresh herbs and vegetables. This school prides itself on using organic ingredients from its own farm, extending an eco-friendly approach to Thai cooking.

What to Expect: A tour of the farm to pick your ingredients, followed by a hands-on cooking class.

Class Price Range: 1,000 – 2,500 THB per person (depending on the class)

Booking: Pre-booking required

3. A Lot of Thai Cooking School

Cuisine: Thai (Specialty: Classic Thai Dishes)

Location: Siri Mangkalajarn Road, near Nimmanhaemin

Overview: A Lot of Thai provides small-group cooking classes, giving you personalized attention. Their classes are designed to teach you how to make authentic Thai dishes, such as Pad Thai, Tom Yum soup, and Green Curry. The classes focus on easy-to-recreate recipes that use fresh and simple ingredients.

What to Expect: A visit to the local market, learning to cook 4-5 different dishes, and enjoying your meal afterward.

Class Price Range: 1,000 – 1,500 THB per person

Booking: Pre-booking recommended

4. Somphong Thai Cooking School

Cuisine: Thai (Specialty: Northern Thai Cuisine)

Location: Nimmanhaemin Road

Overview: Somphong Thai Cooking School provides a more personalized experience with small classes. They emphasize the preparation of traditional Northern Thai dishes. You'll get to cook popular items like Khao Soi (curry noodles) and Sai Oua (Northern Thai sausage).

What to Expect: Instruction on the unique ingredients and techniques used in Northern Thai cooking.

Class Price Range: 1,000 – 1,800 THB per person

Booking: Pre-booking required

5. Cookly

Cuisine: Thai (Variety of Dishes)
Location: Multiple locations across Chiang Mai
Overview: Cookly provides a variety of cooking classes, from street food workshops to traditional Thai cooking classes. They partner with many different cooking schools, so you can choose from different types of classes that suit your preferences. If you're looking for a diverse experience, Cookly is the way to go.
What to Expect: Depending on the tour you choose, it could include a market visit, street food tour, or a full-day cooking workshop.
Class Price Range: 700 – 2,500 THB per person (depending on the tour/class)
Booking: Pre-booking required

6. Chiang Mai Food Tours

Cuisine: Thai (Specialty: Local Street Food)
Location: Various locations across Chiang Mai
Overview: Chiang Mai Food Tours provides guided tours of the city's best street food stalls and hidden eateries. These tours give you the chance to sample local delicacies such as Khao Soi, Sai Oua, and Nam Prik Ong while learning about their history and preparation. The tour guides are local food experts who will introduce

you to some of the city's best-kept culinary secrets.

What to Expect: A guided walking food tour of Chiang Mai's vibrant street food scene, with multiple stops for tastings and insights into the local food culture.

Tour Price Range: 1,200 – 2,000 THB per person

Booking: Pre-booking required

7. Taste of Chiang Mai Food Tours

Cuisine: Thai (Specialty: Authentic Street Food and Market Experiences)

Location: Old City

Overview: This tour provides an authentic Thai food experience by taking you through Chiang Mai's bustling local markets, such as Warorot Market, where you can try local snacks and dishes. You'll also explore the best street food spots around the city, guided by passionate foodies.

What to Expect: A 3-4 hour walking tour, sampling various street food items, learning about their origins, and meeting local vendors.

Tour Price Range: 1,200 – 1,800 THB per person

Booking: Pre-booking recommended

8. Chiang Mai Culinary Arts Centre

Cuisine: Thai (Specialty: Traditional Thai and International Dishes)
Location: Near Nimmanhaemin
Overview: The Chiang Mai Culinary Arts Centre provides both Thai cooking classes and Western culinary classes. The classes are designed for all skill levels and include instructions on essential techniques, such as knife skills and ingredient combinations. This center is ideal for those who want to learn modern Thai cuisine with a fusion twist.
What to Expect: Learn to prepare classic dishes such as Tom Yum Goong, Green Curry, and more, with a modern approach.
Class Price Range: 1,500 – 3,000 THB per person
Booking: Pre-booking required

9. Northern Thai Food and Culture Tour

Cuisine: Northern Thai (Specialty: Khao Soi, Sausages, and Curries)
Location: Various local spots in Chiang Mai
Overview: For a truly immersive experience, the Northern Thai Food and Culture Tour takes you off the beaten path, visiting authentic family-run establishments and learning about

Northern Thai food culture. The tour guides will show you how to make dishes from scratch, using local ingredients.

What to Expect: Visit local food markets, learn how to prepare traditional dishes, and enjoy a meal of your own creations.

Tour Price Range: 1,500 – 3,000 THB per person

Booking: Pre-booking required

Vegetarian and Vegan Dining Options

1. Pun Pun Organic Vegetarian Restaurant

Cuisine: Organic Thai (Specialty: Vegan and Vegetarian Dishes)

Location: Wat Suan Dok area (Near the temple)

Overview: Pun Pun is one of the most well-known spots for organic vegetarian and vegan food in Chiang Mai. They provide a wide range of dishes made from locally sourced, organic ingredients, including curries, stir-fries, and fresh salads. The restaurant is cozy and environmentally conscious, with a focus on sustainability.

Must-Try Dishes: Vegan Pad Thai, Green Curry with Tofu, Larb with Tofu, Spring Rolls, Papaya Salad
Price Range: 100 – 250 THB per dish

2. Free Bird Cafe

Cuisine: Vegetarian, Vegan, and Thai Fusion
Location: Near the Old City
Overview: Free Bird Cafe provides a delightful blend of Thai and Western vegan and vegetarian options. The cafe has a relaxed atmosphere and is known for its delicious, hearty meals and friendly service. The cafe also supports a good cause, as part of its proceeds go to charity, helping people in need across Thailand.
Must-Try Dishes: Vegan Khao Soi, Vegan Thai Green Curry, Burgers, Smoothie Bowls, Raw Desserts
Price Range: 80 – 250 THB per dish

3. The Salad Concept

Cuisine: Vegetarian and Vegan (Specialty: Salads, Smoothies, and Healthy Bowls)
Location: Nimmanhaemin Road
Overview: The Salad Concept is a healthy eatery that focuses on fresh salads, smoothies,

and healthy bowls made from locally sourced vegetables. It's a great spot for those looking for light, nutritious meals. You can create your own salad by choosing from a variety of ingredients or opt for one of their signature bowls.

Must-Try Dishes: Vegan Buddha Bowls, Tropical Smoothie, Acai Bowls, Signature Salads

Price Range: 100 – 200 THB per dish

4. Anchan Vegetarian Restaurant

Cuisine: Thai Vegetarian and Vegan

Location: Siri Mangkalajarn Road

Overview: Anchan serves up delicious vegetarian and vegan Thai food with an emphasis on fresh, local ingredients. The restaurant has a warm and inviting atmosphere, and it's a popular choice for those wanting to try flavorful plant-based versions of traditional Thai dishes.

Must-Try Dishes: Vegan Tom Yum Soup, Vegan Pad Thai, Massaman Curry, Vegetarian Thai Sweets

Price Range: 90 – 250 THB per dish

5. Dada Kafe

Cuisine: Vegetarian, Vegan, and Western Fusion
Location: Old City, near Thapae Gate
Overview: Dada Kafe provides a variety of vegetarian and vegan-friendly dishes, with a focus on healthy, nutrient-packed meals. The restaurant is a favorite among both locals and tourists for its hearty, flavorful options, including smoothies, wraps, and salads. It's a great spot for a light breakfast or lunch.
Must-Try Dishes: Vegan Wraps, Acai Bowl, Vegan Burger, Smoothies
Price Range: 80 – 180 THB per dish

6. Khaomao-Khaofang Restaurant

Cuisine: Thai (Specialty: Vegan and Vegetarian Thai Dishes)
Location: Huay Kaew Road
Overview: Known for its beautiful garden setting, Khaomao-Khaofang provides a wide variety of vegetarian and vegan Thai dishes. The restaurant has an extensive menu with options like curries, soups, and stir-fries, all made from fresh, high-quality ingredients.

Must-Try Dishes: Vegan Massaman Curry, Pad Thai, Fried Tofu with Sweet Chili Sauce, Steamed Rice with Tofu
Price Range: 100 – 250 THB per dish

7. May Kaidee's Vegetarian Restaurant

Cuisine: Thai (Specialty: Vegan and Vegetarian Thai)
Location: Old City
Overview: May Kaidee is a well-loved vegetarian and vegan restaurant in Chiang Mai, famous for its delicious vegan Thai food. It's a great spot for traditional Thai dishes made with plant-based ingredients. They also provide cooking classes, so you can learn how to recreate these dishes at home.
Must-Try Dishes: Vegan Thai Green Curry, Vegan Pad Thai, Curry Noodles, Fresh Spring Rolls
Price Range: 80 – 200 THB per dish

8. The Veganer

Cuisine: Vegan and Vegetarian (Specialty: Vegan Burgers and Sandwiches)
Location: Nimmanhaemin

Overview: The Veganer is a popular vegan restaurant known for its delicious plant-based burgers and sandwiches. In addition to burgers, the menu features bowls, salads, and sides. It's a perfect place for those craving a hearty, vegan take on comfort food.
Must-Try Dishes: Vegan Burgers, Vegan Pizza, Vegan Sandwiches, Vegan Fries
Price Range: 100 – 250 THB per dish

9. Ginger & Kafe

Cuisine: Thai and International (Specialty: Vegetarian and Vegan Options)
Location: Riverside, near the Ping River
Overview: Ginger & Kafe provides a mix of international and Thai cuisine, with a variety of vegetarian and vegan options. This stylish restaurant is known for its delicious fusion dishes, often with a healthy twist. It's a great spot for a cozy dinner or a laid-back lunch.
Must-Try Dishes: Vegan Pad Thai, Vegan Stir-fried Tofu, Ginger and Lemongrass Soup, Vegan Burger
Price Range: 150 – 300 THB per dish

10. Om Garden Cafe

Cuisine: Vegetarian, Vegan, and Raw Food
Location: Nimmanhaemin
Overview: Om Garden Cafe provides an eco-friendly environment with a focus on raw, vegetarian, and vegan dishes. The cafe has a tranquil vibe, making it a perfect spot for health-conscious diners. They provide a variety of smoothies, bowls, and wraps, all made with fresh, plant-based ingredients.
Must-Try Dishes: Raw Pad Thai, Avocado Toast, Smoothie Bowls, Veggie Wraps
Price Range: 100 – 250 THB per dish

SHOPPING AND MARKETS

Night Bazaars and Artisan Markets

1. Chiang Mai Night Bazaar

Location: Chang Klan Road, near the Old City
Opening Hours: Daily from 6:00 PM to 12:00 AM
Overview: The Chiang Mai Night Bazaar is one of the most famous and largest night markets in the city. It's an eclectic mix of everything from clothing, accessories, and home decor to local handicrafts, souvenirs, and street food. This market is a perfect spot to find items such as Thai silk, hand-carved wooden products, hand-painted umbrellas, and local art. It's a bustling, lively place with a vibrant atmosphere.
Must-See Items: Handmade Jewelry, Silk Scarves, Thai Tea Sets, Carved Wooden Statues, Hand-painted Lanterns
Price Range: 100 – 500 THB for most items (though haggling is common and expected)

2. Saturday Night Market (Wua Lai Walking Street)

Location: Wua Lai Road, south of the Old City
Opening Hours: Saturdays from 4:00 PM to 10:00 PM
Overview: The Saturday Night Market is a favorite for those seeking authentic local goods and handcrafted items. It's a bit less touristy than the Night Bazaar, extending a more traditional experience with items like hand-woven fabrics, Thai pottery, and wooden carvings. It's also a fantastic place for food lovers, as the street is lined with food stalls selling local dishes such as khao soi, grilled meats, and Thai sweets.
Must-See Items: Handmade Pottery, Silver Jewelry, Thai Sweets, Traditional Thai Masks
Price Range: 50 – 300 THB for most items

3. Sunday Walking Street Market (Tha Pae Walking Street)

Location: Ratchadamnoen Road, near Tha Pae Gate
Opening Hours: Sundays from 4:00 PM to 10:00 PM

Overview: One of the most popular markets in Chiang Mai, the Sunday Walking Street Market provides a mix of local artisan crafts, street food, and handmade goods. The market stretches along Ratchadamnoen Road, and you'll find everything from handmade clothes, vintage items, leather goods, and original art pieces. This is also a great place to try some authentic Northern Thai snacks such as Sai Oua (a type of sausage) and Khao Niew Ping (sticky rice grilled in banana leaves).

Must-See Items: Handwoven Bags, Thai Clothing, Paintings, Bamboo Crafts, Vegan Snacks

Price Range: 50 – 300 THB for most items

4. Chang Phuak Gate Market

Location: Chang Phuak Gate, north of the Old City

Opening Hours: Nightly, starting from 5:00 PM

Overview: The Chang Phuak Gate Market is a popular spot for both locals and tourists looking for a more authentic night market experience. While this market is primarily focused on street food, you can also find artisan goods such as handmade accessories and local crafts. It's especially famous for its grilled meats, including Khao Kha Moo (braised pork leg over rice).

Must-See Items: Grilled Meats, Sticky Rice Desserts, Silver Jewelry, Handmade Scarves

Price Range: 30 – 150 THB for food, 50 – 200 THB for goods

5. Art in Paradise (3D Art Museum) Market

Location: Chang Klan Road, near the Night Bazaar

Opening Hours: Daily from 10:00 AM to 10:00 PM

Overview: Located near the Chiang Mai Night Bazaar, Art in Paradise also hosts a small artisan market where you can find unique hand-crafted goods inspired by the art museum. This is a great spot for those interested in artistic souvenirs such as paintings, art prints, and sculptures. The market often has local artists showcasing their works alongside traditional Thai handicrafts.

Must-See Items: Hand-painted Canvas Art, Wooden Carvings, Local Sculptures

Price Range: 100 – 1,000 THB, depending on the artwork

6. Anusarn Market

Location: Chang Klan Road (near the Night Bazaar)

Opening Hours: Daily from 6:00 PM to 12:00 AM

Overview: Anusarn Market is a night market that combines both shopping and entertainment. It's home to a variety of artisan stalls selling Thai handicrafts, handmade jewelry, and local art. It's also a lively area with live music, traditional dance performances, and street food vendors. If you're looking for something specific, like silk scarves or bamboo crafts, this market is a great choice.

Must-See Items: Silk Scarves, Wooden Furniture, Thai Tea Sets, Handmade Jewelry

Price Range: 100 – 500 THB for most items

7. Baan Tawai Village (Handicraft Village)

Location: Hang Dong, 15 km south of Chiang Mai

Opening Hours: Daily, 8:00 AM to 6:00 PM (Best visited during the day)

Overview: Baan Tawai is a village known for its woodworking and crafts, and it's the perfect place to shop for unique artisan goods. While not a night market, it is a must-visit for those looking for high-quality wood carvings, furniture, and artisan products. The village is full of workshops where you can watch artisans at work, crafting intricate wooden sculptures, decorative items, and more.

Must-See Items: Wooden Sculptures, Carved Furniture, Thai Ceramics, Handmade Wooden Jewelry

Price Range: 100 – 1,500 THB, depending on the item

8. Local Artisan Markets

Location: Various Locations

Overview: Chiang Mai hosts numerous pop-up artisan markets throughout the year. These markets are held in various locations around the city and feature local artisans showcasing their work. From handmade jewelry and pottery to woven textiles and furniture, these markets are perfect for those who want to bring home something truly special and locally crafted.

Must-See Items: Handcrafted Leather Bags, Pottery, Silk Weavings, Hand-painted Goods

Price Range: 50 – 500 THB for most items

Tips for Shopping at Night Bazaars in Chiang Mai

Bargain: Don't be afraid to haggle, especially at the night markets. Sellers expect it, and you can often get a better deal if you're willing to negotiate.

Bring Cash: Most vendors accept cash (THB), and credit cards might not always be an option, especially at smaller stalls.

Check for Authenticity: Some items, especially those labeled as "handmade," might be mass-produced, so if authenticity is important to you, ask the vendor for details about the item's origin.

Stay Hydrated and Enjoy Local Snacks: The night markets are full of amazing street food, so take breaks to sample local treats like mango sticky rice, fried bananas, and grilled skewers.

Warorot Market Guide

Location:
Warorot Market (also known as Kad Luang) is located in the heart of Chiang Mai, just north of the Ping River, near the Iron Bridge. It's one of the oldest and most bustling markets in the city, extending a wide variety of goods, from fresh produce to local textiles.

Opening Hours:
Daily, from 6:00 AM to 6:00 PM (with some vendors staying open later into the evening)

Overview

Warorot Market is one of the best places to experience the local life and culture of Chiang Mai. This market has a long history, dating back over 100 years, and serves as a hub for both locals and tourists. It provides an authentic, non-touristy shopping experience, where visitors can find everything from traditional Thai snacks and fresh ingredients to clothing and household goods.

The market is divided into several sections, each extending a distinct type of product, and it's a perfect place for those looking to shop for affordable goods, local handicrafts, or to try Northern Thai foods.

What to See and Buy

1. Fresh Produce and Local Ingredients
Warorot is known for its wide selection of fresh fruits, vegetables, herbs, and spices. It's a popular spot for locals to buy ingredients for cooking at home. You'll find a variety of Northern Thai fruits such as longan, lychees, rambutan, and rose apples. The market is also famous for its local herbal medicines and spices used in traditional Thai cooking.
Must-See Items: Fresh herbs, Thai chilies, Exotic fruits (like durian or mangoes in season), Traditional curry pastes

2. Traditional Northern Thai Snacks and Sweets
Warorot is home to many street food stalls where you can sample traditional snacks such as Khao Kha Moo (braised pork leg with rice), Sai Oua (Northern Thai sausage), Nam Prik Ong (spicy tomato dip), and Khao Soi (a rich noodle curry). Local sweets like kanom jeen (fermented rice noodles) and kanom krok (coconut pancakes) are also popular.

Must-Try Foods: Khao Kha Moo, Sai Oua, Khao Soi, Kanom Krok, Sticky Rice with Mango
Price Range: 30 – 150 THB per dish

3. Clothing and Fabrics

Warorot Market is an excellent place to find traditional Thai clothing, especially northern-style fabrics, scarves, and handwoven textiles. It's a great spot to shop for items like silk scarves, skirts, and traditional Thai dress (such as chut thai). You can also find embroidered bags, belts, and shoes.

Must-See Items: Handwoven Fabrics, Silk Scarves, Thai Cotton Shirts, Embroidered Bags
Price Range: 100 – 500 THB

4. Handicrafts and Souvenirs

For those looking for souvenirs, Warorot Market provides a variety of handicrafts like wooden carvings, silver jewelry, and ceramic pieces. You can also find handmade pottery and Thai antiques. The market is a treasure trove of traditional Lanna (Northern Thai) handicrafts and artworks.

Must-See Items: Wooden Carvings, Silver Jewelry, Ceramics, Handmade Pottery
Price Range: 50 – 300 THB for most items

5. Spices and Herbal Products

Warorot Market is a great place to shop for spices and herbal products. You'll find a range of locally grown herbs and spices, which are perfect for anyone looking to recreate the flavors of Chiang Mai at home. The market also has stalls selling essential oils, herbal teas, and traditional remedies.

Must-See Items: Herbal Teas, Essential Oils, Curry Pastes, Dried Flowers and Herbs

Price Range: 50 – 200 THB

6. Household Goods

You'll find an impressive selection of household items at Warorot, from bamboo baskets and wooden kitchen tools to traditional Thai ceramics. The market is a great place for those looking to bring home unique gifts or simply for practical souvenirs to use in daily life.

Must-See Items: Bamboo Baskets, Ceramic Dishes, Wooden Utensils, Traditional Teapots

Price Range: 50 – 500 THB

Street Food and Snacks at Warorot Market

For food lovers, Warorot Market is a paradise. There's a wide variety of street food stalls extending freshly made Khao Kha Moo (braised pork with rice), Sai Oua (Northern Thai sausage), Som Tum (spicy papaya salad), and many more regional dishes. Don't miss out on tasting Khao Soi, Chiang Mai's signature curry noodle dish.

Must-See Foods: Khao Kha Moo, Khao Soi, Sticky Rice with Mango, Grilled Pork Skewers
Price Range: 30 – 100 THB per dish

Tips for Visiting Warorot Market

Arrive Early: Warorot Market is busiest in the mornings and early afternoons, especially for fresh produce, so arriving early will give you the best selection and the least amount of crowds.

Bring Cash: While larger vendors may accept credit cards, it's best to carry cash as most of the smaller stalls only accept it. ATMs are available nearby.

Practice Haggling: Bargaining is a common practice in the market. Don't be afraid to negotiate a better price, especially for souvenirs and clothing.

Bring a Bag: The market can get crowded, and shopping can involve buying multiple items, so bring a sturdy bag for your purchases.

Hydrate and Rest: The market can be hot, especially during the day. Drink plenty of water and take breaks at one of the nearby cafes or food stalls.

How to Get There

By Foot: Warorot Market is located near the Ping River, a short walk from the Iron Bridge and the Night Bazaar. If you're staying in the Old City, it's about a 10-15 minute walk.

By Tuk Tuk: Tuk Tuks are widely available in Chiang Mai, and you can easily take one from the Old City or Nimmanhaemin area to the market.

By Songthaew: Songthaews (red trucks) are a popular form of transportation and will take you to Warorot Market from most parts of Chiang Mai for a reasonable price.

Craft Villages Around Chiang Mai

1. Bo Sang Handicraft Village

Location: Bo Sang, 8 km east of Chiang Mai's Old City

Overview:
Bo Sang Village is world-famous for its handmade umbrellas and parasols. The village's vibrant, colorful umbrellas are crafted from bamboo and sa paper (a local paper made from the mulberry tree). These umbrellas and parasols are intricately painted by hand, showcasing traditional Northern Thai designs, and have become symbolic of Chiang Mai's craft traditions.

What to Do:
Visit local workshops where you can see artisans creating the umbrellas, painting them, and learning the entire process.
Purchase a beautiful umbrella, parasol, or other paper products like fans and hand-painted lanterns.
Attend the Bo Sang Umbrella Festival (held every January), where you can enjoy parades, dance performances, and even try your hand at painting your own umbrella.

Price Range:

Umbrellas and Parasols: 200 – 1,500 THB, depending on size and design

2. San Kamphaeng Handicraft Village

Location: San Kamphaeng, 13 km east of Chiang Mai

Overview:
San Kamphaeng is the hub for Chiang Mai's silk and cotton weaving industry, extending a wide range of textiles, including traditional Lanna fabrics, silk scarves, blankets, and traditional Thai garments. The village is also home to artisans who work with ceramics, silver, and wood, making it an excellent stop for those interested in Northern Thai craftsmanship.

What to Do:
Watch skilled artisans weaving silk and cotton fabrics by hand on traditional looms.
Explore stores selling handwoven textiles, pottery, wood carvings, and silver jewelry.

You can even purchase custom-made items such as silk cushions, scarves, and traditional Thai dresses.

Price Range:
Textiles: 100 – 1,000 THB
Silk Garments: 300 – 2,000 THB

3. Sankampaeng Hot Springs (Pottery Village)

Location: Sankampaeng, 30 km southeast of Chiang Mai

Overview:
While Sankampaeng is known for its hot springs, it is also home to a small but thriving pottery village. Artisans in this village are known for their handcrafted pottery, producing everything from simple cups and bowls to elaborate vases and decorative pieces. The pottery is often made from local clay and fired using traditional techniques.

What to Do:
Visit pottery workshops where you can see artisans creating beautiful pieces from clay, using traditional methods.

Purchase functional pottery such as mugs, bowls, and decorative ceramic pieces that reflect Northern Thai craftsmanship. Take part in pottery-making workshops and create your own souvenirs.

Price Range:
Ceramic Items: 50 – 500 THB, depending on size and design

4. Baan Tawai Village

Location: Baan Tawai, 15 km south of Chiang Mai

Overview:
Baan Tawai is one of the most famous woodworking villages in Thailand, known for its wood carvings, furniture, and sculptures. The village has been producing intricate wooden crafts for generations, including religious carvings, decorative furniture, hand-carved statues, and souvenirs. It's an ideal destination for art lovers and those looking to bring home high-quality wooden goods.

What to Do:
Explore the numerous woodworking workshops where you can see skilled artisans creating beautiful wood carvings by hand.
Browse shops selling high-end wooden furniture, sculptures, and carvings inspired by both Buddhist and Lanna designs.
Visit art galleries where you can purchase one-of-a-kind works of wooden art.

Price Range:
Wooden Carvings: 300 – 3,000 THB
Furniture: 2,000 – 30,000 THB

5. Thung O Village (Silver and Jewelry Crafting)

Location: Thung O, 10 km north of Chiang Mai

Overview:
Thung O is a village known for its fine silver jewelry, and many artisans in this village specialize in creating intricate silver designs, often using traditional techniques. Thung O's silver jewelry is considered among the best in the region, with designs ranging from traditional Thai patterns to more modern styles.

What to Do:
Visit silver workshops where you can watch artisans craft jewelry, from necklaces and bracelets to earrings and rings.
Purchase silver jewelry, which makes for a great souvenir or gift.
Some workshops also provide a chance to try your hand at silver-smithing.

Price Range:
Silver Jewelry: 200 – 5,000 THB, depending on design and craftsmanship

6. Wiang Kum Kam Village (Lanna Art and Artifacts)

Location: Wiang Kum Kam, 5 km south of Chiang Mai's Old City

Overview:
Wiang Kum Kam is not only a historical site but also a place for traditional Lanna art and ceramics. The village is located near ancient ruins and is home to artisans who continue to practice traditional Lanna-style pottery, wood carvings, and silverware. Many visitors come here to buy replicas of ancient artifacts and ceramics inspired by the Lanna kingdom's rich history.

What to Do:

Visit local craft workshops where you can watch the creation of Lanna-style ceramics and pottery.
Buy replica artifacts and ceramic ware from local shops.
Take a guided tour of the archaeological site, which features ruins and ancient temples dating back to the 13th century.

Price Range:
Ceramics: 100 – 500 THB
Lanna Art Replicas: 200 – 1,000 THB

Tips for Visiting Chiang Mai Craft Villages

Buy Directly from Artisans: When possible, purchase goods directly from the artisans. This ensures that they receive fair compensation for their work and gives you an opportunity to learn more about the craft process.
Bargain Respectfully: While bargaining is common in Chiang Mai, it's important to negotiate respectfully. Many prices in these craft villages are set based on the artisan's work, so try to keep the negotiation light and fair.

Bring Cash: Smaller shops in craft villages may not accept credit cards, so make sure to bring cash with you. ATMs are usually available nearby.

Take Your Time: These villages provide a rich cultural experience, so take your time to explore the workshops and interact with the artisans. Many are happy to share their stories and craft processes.

Tips for Bargaining Like a Local

1. Be Friendly and Polite

Smile: A friendly demeanor goes a long way in Thailand. Thai people value politeness and respect, so always approach bargaining with a smile and friendly attitude. This sets a positive tone for negotiations.

Use Simple Phrases in Thai: Learning a few basic Thai words can help establish rapport with vendors. A simple "Sawasdee ka/khrap" (hello) or "Khob khun ka/khrap" (thank you) can show respect and appreciation for their culture.

2. Start with a Lower provide

Begin Low, But Fair: It's common to start at a lower price than what you're willing to pay, but don't go too low, as it might offend the seller. Aim for about 30-40% less than the asking price as your starting point.

Gauge the Vendor's Reaction: Watch the vendor's response to see if you're in the right range. If they seem surprised or insulted, you know you've gone too low, and you can adjust your provide .

3. Show Interest, But Don't Look Too Eager

Don't Appear Desperate: If you show too much enthusiasm for an item, the seller may sense that you're willing to pay more. Browse around first to get an idea of what you're comfortable paying.

Ask for a Discount: If the price isn't marked or if you're buying multiple items, ask directly for a discount. A polite request like, "Can you do a better price if I buy two?" or "What's your best price?" works well.

4. Know the Fair Price Range

Research Before Bargaining: If possible, check prices in nearby stalls or online to get a sense of what items should cost. This can help you avoid being overcharged and give you a realistic idea of what to expect.

Don't Overpay: While you're likely to pay more than the local price, don't let the vendor take advantage of you. Stay within a reasonable price range and avoid buying things that are clearly overpriced.

5. Be Prepared to Walk Away

Don't Be Afraid to Leave: If you're not happy with the price, don't hesitate to walk away. Vendors often call you back with a better provide once they see that you're serious about finding a good deal.

Use Silence as Leverage: After making your provide , sometimes it's best to just stay quiet. The silence can encourage the vendor to provide a better price.

6. Buy Multiple Items for a Discount

Bundle Your Purchases: If you're interested in buying several items, ask for a discount on the total price. Vendors are more likely to give you a better deal if you're purchasing multiple items at once.

Negotiating for More: If you're not getting the price you want on one item, ask for something extra (like a free keychain or small item) as part of the deal.

7. Respect the Seller's Space

Don't Push Too Hard: Bargaining is part of the shopping experience, but it's important to know when to back off. If a vendor is firm on their price and you're not willing to pay, politely decline and move on.

Be Aware of Cultural Sensitivity: Don't use harsh language or aggressive tactics. Always be respectful, as this reflects well on you and ensures the bargaining process remains friendly.

8. Be Patient

Don't Rush: Take your time when bargaining. The seller may take a moment to think about your provide , and rushing can make the process uncomfortable. A relaxed pace helps to maintain good relations. Enjoy the Experience: Bargaining is part of the local shopping culture, so enjoy the process! It's a chance to connect with locals, learn about their crafts, and maybe even share a laugh.

9. Pay in Cash for Better Deals

Cash is King: Many vendors prefer cash over credit cards and might provide a discount if you pay with cash. Be prepared to pay in the local currency (THB), as international cards may not always be accepted.
Smaller Notes Help: Carry smaller denominations to make bargaining easier. Having exact change or close to it can sometimes help you get a better deal, as it saves the vendor from needing to give you change.

10. Don't Feel Obligated to Buy

Don't Force a Deal: If you're not comfortable with the price, there's no need to buy. Sellers understand that not every negotiation will end in a sale, and walking away doesn't mean you've lost.

Buying Authentic Thai Souvenirs

1. Thai Silk and Cotton Products

Chiang Mai is famous for its traditional textiles, particularly silk and cotton. Locally crafted fabrics are known for their vibrant colors and intricate designs, often inspired by the Lanna culture (Northern Thailand's heritage).

What to Buy:
Silk Scarves: Handwoven and dyed silk scarves are lightweight and make for an elegant souvenir.
Cotton Shirts: Soft, comfortable cotton shirts in various colors and patterns, often with traditional Lanna designs.
Traditional Thai Garments: Chang Kben (traditional Thai trousers) and Pha Sin (wrap-around skirts) made from silk or cotton.

Where to Buy:
San Kamphaeng Handicraft Village
Warorot Market
Nimmanhaemin (boutiques and shops specializing in textiles)

Price Range:
Scarves: 150 – 1,500 THB
Shirts: 250 – 1,000 THB

2. Thai Silver Jewelry

Silver has a long history in Thailand, and Chiang Mai is one of the best places to purchase authentic silver jewelry. Skilled artisans in Chiang Mai produce high-quality, handcrafted silver, often with traditional Thai motifs such as lotus flowers and elephants.

What to Buy:
Silver Earrings, Necklaces, and Bracelets
Silver Rings with intricate designs
Traditional Lanna-style Silver Pieces

Where to Buy:

Thung O Village (specializes in silver craftsmanship)
Warorot Market
Baan Tawai Village (well-known for high-quality silver jewelry)

Price Range:
Silver Jewelry: 200 – 5,000 THB depending on design and craftsmanship

3. Hand-Painted Umbrellas from Bo Sang

Bo Sang, a village near Chiang Mai, is famous for its handmade umbrellas and parasols. Crafted from bamboo and sa paper, these colorful umbrellas are intricately painted by hand with designs inspired by nature, traditional patterns, and Buddhist motifs.

What to Buy:
Hand-painted Umbrellas (variety of sizes, colors, and designs)
Hand-painted Fans
Decorative Lanterns

Where to Buy:
Bo Sang Village (where you can see artisans at work)
Handicraft shops in Chiang Mai city

Price Range:
Umbrellas and Parasols: 200 – 1,500 THB
Fans: 50 – 500 THB

4. Thai Wood Carvings

Chiang Mai's wood carving industry is renowned for producing intricate, high-quality wooden pieces that reflect both Thai spirituality and traditional art forms. Items range from decorative sculptures to functional pieces like furniture.

What to Buy:
Wooden Buddha Statues
Intricately Carved Wooden Panels
Traditional Thai Furniture (tables, chairs, and chests)
Wooden Animals and Religious Carvings

Where to Buy:
Baan Tawai Village (center for wooden carvings)
San Kamphaeng Handicraft Village
Local shops around Chiang Mai city

Price Range:
Wooden Statues: 500 – 3,000 THB
Wooden Carvings: 300 – 10,000 THB

5. Thai Pottery and Ceramics

Pottery and ceramics are deeply rooted in Thai culture, with Chiang Mai extending a variety of locally-made ceramic items. You'll find both functional and decorative pieces, often made from local clay and featuring traditional Thai designs.

What to Buy:
Ceramic Tea Sets and Coffee Mugs
Handcrafted Vases and Bowls
Small Figurines and Statue
Thai-style Ceramic Plates

Where to Buy:

Sankampaeng Pottery Village
Wiang Kum Kam Village (Lanna-style pottery)
Local markets in Chiang Mai

Price Range:
Ceramic Mugs: 50 – 200 THB
Vases: 200 – 1,000 THB

6. Thai Tea and Spices

Chiang Mai is a great place to buy authentic Thai teas and spices, which make excellent gifts or souvenirs. Jasmine tea, green tea, and oolong tea are particularly popular, and you can also find locally grown herbs and spices used in Thai cuisine.

What to Buy:
Jasmine Tea and Thai Oolong Tea
Dried Herbs and Spices (lemongrass, chili, kaffir lime leaves)
Curry Paste and Sauces (red curry paste, green curry paste)
Thai Herbal Remedies

Where to Buy:
Warorot Market
Local Specialty Stores in Chiang Mai
Tea shops along Nimmanhaemin

Price Range:
Loose Tea: 100 – 500 THB
Spices and Curry Paste: 50 – 300 THB

7. Thai Massage Oils and Products

Chiang Mai is a haven for traditional Thai massage, and you can bring home a variety of massage oils, balms, and herbal products that are used in Thai wellness practices.

What to Buy:
Herbal Massage Balms
Aromatherapy Oils
Herbal Compresses used in Thai massage
Traditional Thai Soap Bars

Where to Buy:
Warorot Market
Local Wellness Shops in Chiang Mai
Night Bazaars

Price Range:
Massage Oils: 100 – 300 THB
Herbal Compresses: 150 – 500 THB

8. Handwoven Baskets and Bags

Chiang Mai is also known for its beautifully crafted handwoven baskets, bags, and other accessories made from bamboo, rattan, and cotton. These items showcase Thai craftsmanship and make for both practical and decorative souvenirs.

What to Buy:
Handwoven Baskets
Cotton Handbags and Tote Bags
Woven Wallets and Purses

Where to Buy:
Handicraft Villages (especially San Kamphaeng and Bo Sang)
Warorot Market
Nimmanhaemin boutiques

Price Range:
Baskets and Bags: 150 – 1,000 THB

9. Traditional Thai Musical Instruments

For a unique souvenir, look for traditional Thai musical instruments, such as khim (hammered dulcimer), ranat (xylophone), and pi (reed instruments). These instruments are deeply embedded in Thai culture and can be a special reminder of your time in Chiang Mai.

What to Buy:
Khim (hammered dulcimer)

Ranat (Thai xylophone)
Pi (traditional Thai reed instruments)

Where to Buy:
Chiang Mai Night Bazaar
Specialty Shops near Cultural Centers

Price Range:
Small Instruments: 300 – 1,500 THB
Larger Instruments: 2,000 – 10,000 THB

Tips for Buying Souvenirs in Chiang Mai

Bargain Respectfully: As mentioned earlier, bargaining is common, but always remain respectful and friendly. Sellers appreciate polite customers and are often willing to provide discounts for a positive exchange.
Look for Authenticity: Check the authenticity of items, especially textiles and wood carvings, to ensure you're purchasing genuine local crafts.
Buy Local Products: Opt for souvenirs that are handmade by local artisans, as this supports the local economy and provides a more authentic experience.
Pack Carefully: Some items like pottery, silk, or wood carvings can be fragile, so ensure you pack them securely or ask vendors for advice on how to pack them for travel.

DAY TRIPS AND EXCURSIONS

Chiang Rai and the White Temple

Chiang Rai, located about 3-4 hours north of Chiang Mai, is a charming city that provides some of Thailand's most extraordinary and unique attractions, including the iconic Wat Rong Khun (the White Temple). A day trip from Chiang Mai to Chiang Rai is a must for travelers looking to explore the region's artistic and cultural marvels.

How to Get to Chiang Rai from Chiang Mai

To visit Chiang Rai, travelers typically take either a bus, private car, or join a guided tour.

By Bus: Buses from the Chiang Mai Arcade Bus Station depart regularly and take around 3.5 to 4 hours to reach Chiang Rai. The ticket price is generally between 150 – 300 THB, depending on the bus company and class of service.
By Private Car: Hiring a private car or taxi is a more comfortable option and takes around 3 hours. A round-trip price for a private car can range from 2,000 – 4,000 THB, depending on the type of vehicle.

Guided Tours: Many tour companies in Chiang Mai provide day trips to Chiang Rai that include transportation, a guide, and visits to the White Temple and other notable spots in the area. Prices for these tours typically range from 1,000 – 3,000 THB per person, including lunch and entrance fees.

The White Temple (Wat Rong Khun)

One of the most famous landmarks in Chiang Rai, Wat Rong Khun (commonly known as the White Temple), is a stunning contemporary Buddhist temple designed by Thai artist Chalermchai Kositpipat. The temple, completed in the early 21st century, is renowned for its dazzling white color, intricate artwork, and surreal designs.

What Makes the White Temple Unique

White Color and Mirrors: The temple is entirely white, symbolizing the purity of Buddha. It's adorned with mirrored glass, which reflects light and gives the temple an ethereal, almost otherworldly appearance.
Iconic Architecture: The temple features intricate carvings and surreal artwork that blend traditional Buddhist iconography with

modern, pop-culture elements. You'll see depictions of Hell, Heaven, and figures like superheroes and film characters, which gives the temple an avant-garde feel.

The Bridge of the "Cycle of Rebirth": Upon entering the temple, visitors cross a bridge that symbolizes the passage from the cycle of rebirth (represented by hands reaching up from the ground) to the spiritual enlightenment provide ed within the temple itself.

The Golden Bathroom: Another feature of the White Temple is a small structure known as the Golden Bathroom, which stands in stark contrast to the white temple but continues the surreal theme.

Visiting the White Temple

Entry Fee: The entrance fee is around 50 THB for foreigners. Some areas, like the art gallery, might require an additional fee.

Opening Hours: The temple is open from 8:00 AM to 5:00 PM, but it's best to arrive early to avoid crowds, especially if you want to take photos without many people in the background.

Dress Code: While there is no strict dress code, visitors should dress modestly when visiting the temple. Avoid wearing shorts or sleeveless tops as a sign of respect.

Other Attractions in Chiang Rai

While the White Temple is the highlight of Chiang Rai, there are several other fascinating spots to explore in the area:

1. The Blue Temple (Wat Rong Suea Ten)

Another stunning temple in Chiang Rai is the Blue Temple (Wat Rong Suea Ten). It is known for its vibrant blue color and intricate gold details. The temple features striking modern art, including a large white Buddha statue, which provides a unique contrast to the more traditional temples of Thailand.

Entry Fee: Free
Opening Hours: 8:00 AM – 5:00 PM

2. The Golden Triangle

The Golden Triangle is where the borders of Thailand, Laos, and Myanmar meet. It is a historically significant area, once known for its involvement in the opium trade. You can take a boat ride on the Mekong River to see the confluence of the three countries and visit the nearby Opium Museum to learn about the region's opium history.

Boat Ride Price: 200 – 400 THB (per person)
Opium Museum Entry Fee: 40 – 50 THB

3. Baan Dam (Black House)

Baan Dam, also known as the Black House, is an unusual and thought-provoking museum created by Thai artist Thawan Duchanee. It features a collection of black wooden structures filled with strange, sometimes eerie, artwork and sculptures that blend traditional Thai craftsmanship with dark themes.

Entry Fee: 80 THB
Opening Hours: 9:00 AM – 5:00 PM

Pai

Nestled in the mountains of northern Thailand, Pai is a small, laid-back town in Mae Hong Son Province, located about 3 hours from Chiang Mai. Known for its stunning natural beauty, relaxed atmosphere, and vibrant cultural scene, Pai has become a popular destination for travelers seeking a peaceful retreat, adventure, and a taste of rural Thai life.

How to Get to Pai from Chiang Mai

By Bus: The most common way to get to Pai is by bus from Chiang Mai's Arcade Bus Station. The journey takes around 3 hours, and the price typically ranges from 150 – 250 THB for a one-way ticket. Be prepared for winding mountain roads, which may make the trip a bit challenging for those prone to motion sickness.

By Private Car or Taxi: Hiring a private car or taxi can provide a more comfortable and quicker option, with prices ranging from 2,500 – 4,000 THB for a one-way trip. The drive provides scenic views of the mountains and valleys.

By Motorcycle/Scooter: For the more adventurous, renting a motorcycle or scooter is a popular way to reach Pai. The journey takes around 3 hours, and scooter rentals cost around 200 – 350 THB per day.

Best Time to Visit Pai

The best time to visit Pai is during the cool season (November to February), when the weather is mild, and the landscape is lush and green. This is also the peak tourist season, so Pai can be busier, especially during the holidays. However, if you're looking for a quieter experience, the shoulder season (March to May) provides warm weather and fewer crowds.

Cool Season: November to February (ideal for outdoor activities)
Hot Season: March to May (ideal for those who prefer fewer tourists)
Rainy Season: June to October (lush greenery but can be challenging for travel)

Things to Do in Pai

1. Pai Canyon (Kong Lan)

Pai Canyon is one of the most popular attractions in the area. The canyon features narrow, winding trails with dramatic cliffs and stunning views of the surrounding mountains and valleys. It's a great place for a short hike, especially at sunset when the canyon is bathed in golden light.

Entry Fee: Free
Best Time to Visit: Sunset (for the best views)

2. Hot Springs

Pai is home to several natural hot springs, perfect for a relaxing soak in nature. Tha Pai Hot Springs is the most famous and is located about 8 kilometers from Pai town. The hot springs are surrounded by lush jungle, creating a serene atmosphere.

Entry Fee: 20 – 300 THB (depending on the spring)
Best Time to Visit: Early morning or late afternoon (to avoid crowds)

3. Bamboo Bridge (Sang Kha Yai Bridge)

The Bamboo Bridge is a scenic wooden bridge that stretches across rice fields and is a great spot for a leisurely walk and photo opportunities. It's located just outside Pai town, and you can enjoy the beautiful rural landscapes as you walk along the bridge.

Entry Fee: Free

Best Time to Visit: Sunrise or sunset for beautiful lighting

4. Pai Walking Street

Pai's Walking Street is a vibrant market that takes place every evening. The street is lined with stalls selling local handicrafts, clothing, food, and souvenirs. It's also a great place to enjoy local street food, including grilled meats, fresh fruit smoothies, and local desserts.

Best Time to Visit: Evening (4:00 PM – 10:00 PM)

5. Pai Land Split

Pai Land Split is an interesting natural phenomenon where the ground literally cracked open, creating a large gap in the earth. The owners of the site have turned it into a small tourist attraction, extending fresh fruit and homemade juice for visitors. It's a great spot for photos and learning about the area's geology.

Entry Fee: 50 THB
Best Time to Visit: Morning or afternoon (before it gets too hot)

6. Waterfalls

Pai is home to several beautiful waterfalls, which are perfect for a refreshing dip on a hot day. Some of the most popular ones include:

Mo Paeng Waterfall: A multi-tiered waterfall where you can swim and relax.
Pam Bok Waterfall: A quieter, less crowded waterfall with crystal-clear pools.

Entry Fee: Free
Best Time to Visit: Rainy season (for the most dramatic falls)

7. Visit a Local Hill Tribe Village

Pai is surrounded by various hill tribes, including the Karen, Hmong, and Lisu tribes. Many tours from Pai provide the opportunity to visit these villages to learn about the traditional lifestyles, crafts, and cultures of these indigenous groups.

Tour Prices: 500 – 1,500 THB (depending on the tour length and inclusions)

8. Explore Pai's Cafes and Eateries

Pai has a thriving food scene, with many quirky cafes and restaurants that cater to different tastes. From organic eateries and vegan restaurants to coffee shops with beautiful views, you'll find plenty of places to enjoy a relaxing meal or coffee. Some notable spots include:

Café de Pai: Known for its picturesque setting and organic food.

The Curry Shack: provides great Indian food, including curries and naan.

Pai's Coffee: Ideal for coffee lovers, serving locally roasted coffee.

Where to Stay in Pai

Budget Hostels: Prices range from 150 – 400 THB per night. Options like Pai Circus School Hostel and SpicyPai Backpackers provide affordable stays and a social atmosphere.

Mid-Range Hotels: Prices range from 600 – 1,500 THB per night. Pai Village Boutique Resort & Farm and Pai River Lodge are popular choices extending comfort with a touch of luxury.

Luxury Resorts: Prices range from 2,000 – 4,000 THB per night. Reverie Siam Resort and Pai Resort are great options for a more upscale experience.

Pai's Unique Vibe

Pai is often described as a place where time slows down. The town has a bohemian and artistic vibe, attracting backpackers, digital nomads, and travelers seeking a peaceful retreat. Whether you spend your days hiking, visiting temples, or simply relaxing by the river, Pai provides a unique and laid-back escape from the hustle and bustle of city life.

Mae Hong Son Loop

Overview of the Mae Hong Son Loop

Total Distance: Approximately 600 kilometers (370 miles)
Time Required: 3 to 5 days, depending on your pace and the number of stops you make

Route:

Start in Chiang Mai
Travel to Pai
Continue to Mae Hong Son
Head towards Soppong or Pang Mapha
Return to Chiang Mai

Best Time to Drive the Mae Hong Son Loop

Cool Season (November to February): Ideal for road trips with comfortable temperatures and clear skies. The cool season is the peak tourist time, so you may find more visitors.
Hot Season (March to May): The weather is warm, and the roads can get dusty, but it's less crowded.

Rainy Season (June to October): The rainy season can make travel a bit challenging due to slippery roads and possible flooding, especially in remote areas. However, the landscape is lush and green, which is great for nature lovers.

Highlights of the Mae Hong Son Loop

1. Chiang Mai to Pai

The journey from Chiang Mai to Pai is a classic road trip adventure, covering around 130 kilometers. The winding roads through the mountains provide incredible scenic views, but also require careful driving.

What to Do in Pai:

Visit Pai Canyon, Pai Walking Street, and Tha Pai Hot Springs.
Explore the Bamboo Bridge and enjoy the peaceful rural landscapes.
Relax and unwind in one of the many charming cafes or restaurants.

2. Pai to Mae Hong Son

From Pai, the road to Mae Hong Son is about 110 kilometers. This part of the loop features breathtaking landscapes, passing through hills, valleys, and dense forests.

What to Do in Mae Hong Son:

Visit Wat Phra That Doi Kong Mu, a hilltop temple with panoramic views of the city and surrounding mountains.
Explore Pang Ung, known as the "Switzerland of Thailand," a picturesque lake surrounded by pine trees.
Take a boat ride on Pai River and enjoy the serene environment.
Discover the local hill tribes and their traditional villages.

3. Mae Hong Son to Soppong (Pang Mapha)

After Mae Hong Son, head towards Soppong, a village that is part of the Pang Mapha district. This area is less touristy and is great for nature lovers and adventurers.

What to Do in Soppong/Pang Mapha:

Explore the Tham Lod Cave, a large limestone cave system with prehistoric art and river passages that can be explored by boat.

Visit the Bamboo Bridge over the Soppong River.

If you have time, hike through the forest to spot wildlife, or take a local guide to visit nearby hill tribe villages.

4. Soppong to Chiang Mai

From Soppong, make your way back to Chiang Mai. The drive is about 200 kilometers and provides more opportunities for scenic stops and exploration.

What to Expect Along the Mae Hong Son Loop

Mountain Roads: The Mae Hong Son Loop is famous for its winding roads and sharp turns. There are 1,864 curves along the loop, making it an exhilarating yet challenging drive. Some stretches can be quite steep, so make sure your vehicle is in good condition.
Beautiful Scenery: Expect dramatic landscapes, including lush valleys, rivers, waterfalls, forests, and mountains. The region is known for its natural beauty and is a photographer's paradise.
Local Culture: Along the loop, you'll pass through traditional hill tribe villages where you

can learn about the culture and lifestyle of the local people. Some of these communities are the Karen, Hmong, Lahu, and Lisu tribes.

Tips for the Mae Hong Son Loop

Rent a Motorcycle or Car: Renting a motorcycle or car is the most popular way to explore the loop. Rental prices typically range from 200 – 350 THB/day for a scooter and 1,000 – 2,000 THB/day for a car.

Be Prepared for Curvy Roads: If you're driving a motorcycle, make sure you're comfortable with winding roads. The roads can be steep and challenging, especially during the rainy season when they can get slippery.

Fuel Up: There are petrol stations along the loop, but it's a good idea to fill up your tank when you can, especially in more remote areas.

Weather Conditions: The weather in the mountains can change rapidly, so bring layers, sunscreen, and a raincoat, especially if you're traveling during the rainy season.

Accommodation: There are plenty of accommodations along the route, from budget hostels and guesthouses to more luxurious resorts. Booking in advance is recommended, particularly during the high season.

Hot Springs and Cave Exploration in Chiang Dao

Chiang Dao, a town located about 70 kilometers north of Chiang Mai, is known for its natural beauty, including its hot springs, limestone caves, and surrounding mountains. This area is a great destination for travelers seeking adventure and relaxation. Whether you're interested in a soothing dip in a hot spring or exploring a vast cave system, Chiang Dao provides plenty of opportunities for both.

Hot Springs in Chiang Dao

Chiang Dao is home to several natural hot springs, known for their therapeutic qualities. These hot springs are surrounded by beautiful natural landscapes, making them a perfect place to relax after a day of exploration.

1. Chiang Dao Hot Springs

The Chiang Dao Hot Springs is the most famous hot spring in the area. Located at the foot of Doi Chiang Dao, this natural hot spring features a large pool where visitors can relax in the warm waters. The water is rich in minerals and is believed to have healing properties. The hot spring is located in a beautiful setting, surrounded by lush greenery and the sounds of nature.

Facilities: There are both public and private hot spring pools, with some private pools available for rent if you prefer more privacy.

Activities: You can soak in the natural hot spring water or try the egg-boiling activity, where you can boil eggs in the hot spring's water.

Entrance Fee: Around 20 – 50 THB for the public pool; private pools may cost more.

Best Time to Visit: Early morning or late afternoon to avoid crowds and enjoy the peaceful atmosphere.

2. Fang Hot Springs (Near Chiang Dao)

Located a bit further north, in Fang, the Fang Hot Springs is another excellent spot for visitors looking to experience thermal waters. Though not as well-known as the Chiang Dao Hot Springs, it provides a peaceful setting and is less crowded.

Facilities: Public and private soaking pools with clean facilities.
Entrance Fee: Around 50 – 100 THB.
Best Time to Visit: Morning or evening, particularly during cooler months.

Cave Exploration in Chiang Dao

Chiang Dao is also home to Chiang Dao Cave, one of the largest and most impressive limestone caves in Thailand. The cave system is located at the foot of Doi Chiang Dao, Thailand's third-highest mountain, and provides a fascinating glimpse into the natural beauty and geological history of the region.

1. Chiang Dao Cave (Tham Chiang Dao)

The Chiang Dao Cave is the main attraction for cave enthusiasts. The cave consists of several chambers, some of which are adorned with stunning stalactites and stalagmites. The cave is believed to be over 1,000 years old and holds significant religious importance to local people, as there are small shrines and Buddha statues inside.

Tour Options: You can either explore the cave on your own or hire a local guide to show you

around. Guides are available at the cave entrance for a small fee and can help you explore the more hidden parts of the cave.
Entrance Fee: Approximately 40 – 100 THB, depending on the areas you wish to explore.
Opening Hours: The cave is open daily from 8:00 AM to 4:00 PM.
What to Expect: Inside, you'll find several chambers filled with impressive rock formations. Some parts of the cave require climbing or squeezing through narrow passages. There's also a small temple inside where locals come to worship.

2. Pha Daeng Cave

Located near the Chiang Dao Cave, Pha Daeng Cave is another great option for those seeking a less crowded experience. This cave is less developed and requires some hiking to reach the entrance, but it rewards visitors with a sense of adventure and the opportunity to see fewer tourists.
What to Expect: The cave is more rustic and wild, with fewer man-made improvements, which makes it ideal for those looking for a more authentic and natural cave experience.
Entry Fee: Free (though a small donation for maintenance is appreciated).

Best Time to Visit: Morning, to avoid the midday heat and crowds.

How to Get to Chiang Dao

By Car: Chiang Dao is about 1.5 to 2 hours north of Chiang Mai. You can rent a car or hire a taxi for around 1,500 – 2,500 THB one-way.

By Bus: Buses from Chiang Mai's Arcade Bus Station depart for Chiang Dao regularly. The journey takes about 2 hours and costs around 50 – 100 THB.

By Scooter: For the more adventurous, renting a scooter is a great way to explore the area. Expect to pay around 200 – 350 THB per day.

NIGHTLIFE AND ENTERTAINMENT

Rooftop Bars and Live Music Venues

Rooftop Bars

1. Sky Bar at Akyra Manor Chiang Mai

Located on the top floor of Akyra Manor in the stylish Nimmanhaemin area, the Sky Bar provides panoramic views of the city, especially at sunset. It's an ideal place to enjoy a cocktail while overlooking the rolling hills and city skyline.
Ambiance: Chic and trendy, with a laid-back vibe perfect for enjoying evening drinks.
Signature Drinks: The bar serves creative cocktails, fine wines, and a variety of refreshing beverages.
Best For: Sunset views and stylish city views.
Price Range: Cocktails around 250 – 350 THB.

2. The Roof at Hotel M Chiang Mai

Situated on the rooftop of Hotel M Chiang Mai, this bar provides a fantastic 360-degree view of the Old City and Doi Suthep. It's a more relaxed venue, great for those who want to enjoy a drink in a peaceful environment.

Ambiance: Casual and contemporary, with cozy seating and a laid-back atmosphere.

Signature Drinks: A mix of cocktails, beer, and mocktails.

Best For: Enjoying views of the Old City and mountains.

Price Range: Cocktails around 200 – 300 THB.

3. The Social@26

Located on the top floor of Le Méridien Chiang Mai, The Social@26 provides an upscale ambiance with impressive views of the surrounding mountains and cityscape. The venue is known for its stylish decor and excellent selection of drinks.

Ambiance: Elegant, with contemporary décor and intimate lighting.

Signature Drinks: Signature cocktails, wine list, and craft beers.

Best For: Romantic evenings and upscale nightlife.

Price Range: Cocktails around 250 – 350 THB.

4. The Riverside Bar & Restaurant

Although not exactly on a rooftop, The Riverside Bar & Restaurant is located along the Ping River and provides a stunning outdoor setting with great views of the river, especially during sunset and at night.
Ambiance: Relaxed, with live music and a picturesque riverside location.
Signature Drinks: A wide variety of cocktails, local beers, and refreshing drinks.
Best For: Riverfront views and casual dining.
Price Range: Cocktails around 150 – 250 THB.

Live Music Venues

1. The North Gate Jazz Co-Op

One of Chiang Mai's most famous live music venues, The North Gate Jazz Co-Op is located near the Old City. This cozy venue hosts some of the best jazz performances in the city, featuring local and international musicians.
Ambiance: Relaxed, intimate, and music-focused, with a great local crowd.
Music Style: Live jazz, ranging from smooth jazz to Latin and fusion styles.

Best For: Jazz lovers and a laid-back music experience.
Cover Charge: Typically around 100 – 150 THB.

2. The Beer Republic

A popular expat spot in Chiang Mai, The Beer Republic provides live music almost every night. It's a fun, social venue where you can enjoy a cold drink while listening to a variety of local and traveling bands.
Ambiance: Lively, with a friendly, energetic vibe.
Music Style: Rock, pop, and local acoustic performances.
Best For: A vibrant night out with friends and live band music.
Cover Charge: Free entry, with food and drinks priced around 100 – 300 THB.

3. Zoe in Yellow

Located in the heart of the Old City, Zoe in Yellow is a favorite among tourists and locals alike. Known for its lively atmosphere, this venue has a mix of live music, DJs, and dancing, creating a festive vibe.

Ambiance: Vibrant, with a club-like feel.
Music Style: Mix of live music, DJs, and dance music.
Best For: Party-goers and those seeking a lively night out.
Cover Charge: Typically 50 – 100 THB, depending on the event.

4. Cat House

For a more laid-back and intimate music experience, Cat House provides live acoustic performances in a cozy setting. It's a small venue with a relaxed, friendly atmosphere, ideal for a more personal music experience.
Ambiance: Cozy and chill, with soft lighting and a laid-back crowd.
Music Style: Acoustic, folk, and indie performances.
Best For: A chill evening of acoustic tunes and good vibes.
Cover Charge: Free entry.

5. The Smiling Pub

A well-established live music venue in Chiang Mai, The Smiling Pub has been around for decades and is a great spot for both locals and tourists to enjoy live music in a cozy setting.

Ambiance: Casual and friendly, with an old-school pub feel.

Music Style: A variety of genres, from rock to pop and classic hits.

Best For: A laid-back night out with live music and drinks.

Cover Charge: Around 50 – 100 THB.

Tips for Enjoying Rooftop Bars and Live Music Venues in Chiang Mai

Dress Code: Some rooftop bars may have a smart-casual dress code, so it's best to avoid wearing flip-flops or overly casual clothing at upscale venues.

Peak Hours: Rooftop bars can get crowded around sunset, so it's a good idea to arrive early if you want to grab a good spot to enjoy the view.

Reservation: For popular live music venues, particularly those with famous bands or special events, it's advisable to make a reservation in advance.

Cover Charges: While many live music venues in Chiang Mai are free to enter, some may have a cover charge, especially for special performances or events. Be sure to check in advance.

Cash vs Card: Most places accept credit cards, but it's always a good idea to carry cash, especially at smaller venues or bars.

Chiang Mai's Night Markets

1. The Sunday Walking Street (Ratchadamnoen Road)

Arguably Chiang Mai's most famous night market, the Sunday Walking Street is a must-visit for tourists and locals alike. This bustling market stretches along Ratchadamnoen Road, right through the Old City, and transforms into a pedestrian paradise every Sunday evening.

What to Expect:
Handmade crafts, jewelry, and textiles, many of which are created by local artisans.
Street food stalls extending authentic Thai snacks
like pad thai, mango sticky rice, and grilled meats.
Live music and street performers create a festive atmosphere.

Traditional Thai goods, including Thai silk, herbal products, and souvenirs.
Best For: Finding unique souvenirs and experiencing the lively energy of the city.
Opening Hours: 4:00 PM – 10:00 PM, Sundays only.
Location: Ratchadamnoen Road, Old City.

2. The Saturday Night Market (Wua Lai Road)

Similar to the Sunday Walking Street but with its own distinct character, the Saturday Night Market is held along Wua Lai Road, just south of the Old City. It's a great option if you're in Chiang Mai on a Saturday and want to explore a more relaxed, but equally charming market.

What to Expect:
A similar mix of handmade crafts and local art.
Delicious food stalls serving Thai and international cuisine, including vegetarian and vegan options.
Street musicians and performances showcasing local talent.
Plenty of clothing and accessories, from trendy items to traditional Thai wear.

Best For: A quieter, less crowded version of the Sunday Walking Street.

Opening Hours: 4:00 PM – 10:00 PM, Saturdays only.
Location: Wua Lai Road, just south of the Old City.

3. The Night Bazaar (Chang Klan Road)

For a more traditional night market experience, the Night Bazaar on Chang Klan Road is one of the most popular in Chiang Mai. Open every evening, this market is a lively shopping hub where you can find just about anything — from clothing and accessories to souvenirs and electronics.

What to Expect:
Large variety of goods ranging from local handicrafts and clothing to mass-produced souvenirs.
Street food vendors serving up delicious Thai snacks, including satay, spring rolls, and fresh fruit.
Thai massage parlors where you can relax after a busy day of shopping.
Bargaining opportunities — the Night Bazaar is a great place to haggle for items.

Best For: Shopping for souvenirs and experiencing a bustling Thai market.
Opening Hours: 6:00 PM – Midnight, every night.
Location: Chang Klan Road, near the eastern part of the Old City.

4. Anusarn Market

Located just behind the Night Bazaar, Anusarn Market is another fantastic night market in Chiang Mai. It's often less crowded than the main Night Bazaar, making it a more relaxed experience. However, it still provides a great selection of goods, food, and entertainment.

What to Expect:
Handmade jewelry, textiles, and woodwork crafted by local artisans.
Delicious street food, such as fresh seafood, Thai noodles, and ice cream.
Live performances by Thai musicians and dancers.
Art galleries and shops selling local artwork and crafts.

Best For: A quieter, less touristy shopping experience with plenty of entertainment.

Opening Hours: 5:00 PM – 11:00 PM, every night.
Location: Chang Klan Road, near the Night Bazaar.

5. The Sunday Night Market at Thapae Gate

A vibrant extension of the Sunday Walking Street market, the Sunday Night Market at Thapae Gate provides a mix of food, clothing, and souvenirs, along with street performances. It's located at one of the most iconic spots in the Old City — Thapae Gate.

What to Expect:
Cultural performances by local artists.
Authentic Thai food, from grilled skewers to coconut ice cream.
Handmade goods like locally crafted bags, jewelry, and pottery.

Best For: A cultural experience in the heart of the Old City.
Opening Hours: 4:00 PM – 10:00 PM, Sundays only.
Location: Thapae Gate, Old City.

6. Kalare Night Market

Kalare Night Market is located near the Night Bazaar and provides a mix of traditional Thai handicrafts, food, and entertainment. It's a great place for tourists looking to sample local delicacies or shop for unique gifts.

What to Expect:
Traditional Thai crafts, such as pottery, textiles, and wood carvings.
Indoor food court with a variety of Thai dishes, including fried rice, noodles, and curries.
Massages and spa treatments available to unwind after shopping.

Best For: A quieter alternative to the Night Bazaar, with more focus on food.
Opening Hours: 6:00 PM – Midnight, every night.
Location: Kalare Night Market, near the Night Bazaar.

7. The Flower Market (Siam Road)

While not strictly a "night market," the Flower Market (also known as Ton Lamyai Market) is especially active in the evening when it comes alive with vibrant colors and fresh scents.

Located near the Night Bazaar, this market is a great place to explore Thai floriculture.

What to Expect:
A huge selection of flowers, including orchids, roses, and marigolds, commonly used in Thai Buddhist ceremonies.
Fresh fruits and herbal products sold alongside flowers.
Traditional garlands used for extending s at temples.

Best For: Those interested in seeing the floral beauty of Chiang Mai and the local tradition of flower extending .
Opening Hours: 5:00 PM – 11:00 PM, every night.
Location: Siam Road, near the Night Bazaar.

Shopping Tips for Chiang Mai's Night Markets

Bargaining: Bargaining is part of the fun in Chiang Mai's markets, so don't be afraid to negotiate prices. Start by extending around 50% of the initial asking price and work from there.
Cash: Most markets operate on a cash-only basis, so make sure to carry enough Thai Baht.

ATMs are available, but you might want to avoid the fees by withdrawing cash in advance. Timings: While markets like the Night Bazaar are open every night, others like the Sunday Walking Street are only held on specific days, so plan your visit accordingly.

Be Prepared for Crowds: Especially on weekends, markets like the Sunday Walking Street can get crowded. If you prefer a more relaxed experience, try visiting on weekdays or earlier in the evening.

Nightclubs and Dance Spots

1. Zoe in Yellow

One of Chiang Mai's most popular nightlife spots, Zoe in Yellow is a club where the young, hip crowd gathers to party until late. Located in the heart of the Old City, this club provides an energetic vibe, great music, and a fun atmosphere.

What to Expect:
Electronic dance music (EDM) and house beats played by local and international DJs.

A large outdoor area for those who prefer dancing under the stars.

Themed nights with events and promotions.
A mix of local Thais and tourists, making it a lively spot for mingling.

Best For: Party lovers looking for a lively, energetic environment.
Opening Hours: 9:00 PM – Late, every night.
Location: Old City, near Thapae Gate.

2. The Warm Up Café

Known as one of the city's longest-running nightlife venues, The Warm Up Café is a favorite among locals and tourists alike. Located on Nimmanhaemin Road, this spot provides a mix of live music and club-style vibes with a spacious dance floor.

What to Expect:
A mix of live performances (local bands, acoustic sets) and DJ nights playing popular hits.
A variety of Thai and international music, including pop, hip-hop, and electronic.
Chilled-out seating areas, perfect for those who want to take a break from dancing.

A great spot to experience Chiang Mai's local nightlife culture.

Best For: A mix of live music and dancing with a local crowd.
Opening Hours: 8:00 PM – Late, every night.
Location: Nimmanhaemin Road.

3. Spicy

For a more intense party experience, Spicy is a well-known nightclub in Chiang Mai where the beats go late into the night. It's one of the city's most popular spots for those who enjoy an electronic music scene.

What to Expect:
EDM and techno music, with DJ sets playing the latest hits.
A crowd of backpackers, locals, and tourists who enjoy partying until the early hours of the morning.
Themed parties with special events and guest DJs.
A more underground vibe with dark lighting and neon decor.

Best For: Hardcore partygoers and lovers of EDM.

Opening Hours: 9:00 PM – 2:00 AM, every night.

Location: Soi 7, close to the Night Bazaar.

4. Infinity Club

Infinity Club is one of Chiang Mai's upscale nightclubs, extending a chic and modern environment for clubbing. Located in the Nimmanhaemin area, it's a great spot for those looking to dance in style.

What to Expect:
International DJs and regular themed parties with EDM, house, and hip-hop.
A luxury nightclub experience with VIP sections and bottle service.
A stylish and upscale crowd, perfect for those who want a more glamorous night out.
A state-of-the-art sound system and lighting design that creates an exciting atmosphere.

Best For: Those seeking a more upscale, trendy nightclub experience.

Opening Hours: 10:00 PM – Late, every night.
Location: Nimmanhaemin Road.

5. Brix Club

For those who enjoy a more intimate and alternative vibe, Brix Club provides a unique nightclub experience in Chiang Mai. Known for its welcoming atmosphere, this spot draws a mix of expats, locals, and travelers.

What to Expect:
A variety of dance genres, including house, hip-hop, and occasional live bands.
A laid-back and chill vibe, with a smaller but energetic crowd.
Outdoor seating areas for a more relaxed experience when not dancing.
Craft cocktails and a fun mix of locals and tourists.

Best For: People looking for an intimate yet energetic dance experience.
Opening Hours: 9:00 PM – Late, every night.
Location: Near Nimmanhaemin.

6. The Riverside Bar & Restaurant

While not a traditional nightclub, The Riverside provides a great place to enjoy drinks, live music, and dance, especially for those who prefer a more relaxed environment before heading to a club. It's located near the Ping River, making it one of the most scenic spots in the city.

What to Expect:
Live music performances, ranging from acoustic sets to upbeat dance tracks.
A large dance floor, especially during weekends when the crowd is more lively.
Great cocktails and a riverside view, adding a more laid-back, scenic experience.

Best For: Enjoying live music and a dancefloor in a relaxed setting.
Opening Hours: 6:00 PM – 1:00 AM, every night.
Location: 9/1 Charoenprathet Road, Riverside.

7. The North Gate Jazz Co-Op

While not a dance club per se, The North Gate Jazz Co-Op is a must-visit for music lovers, especially for those who enjoy live jazz. It's a popular spot for both locals and tourists, providing an energetic vibe with music that often leads to spontaneous dancing.

What to Expect:
Live jazz performances by local and international musicians.
A vibrant, eclectic crowd, many of whom enjoy dancing to the live music.
A casual, artistic atmosphere, perfect for a laid-back night out with a touch of energy.

Best For: Jazz lovers and those looking for a more relaxed dance experience.
Opening Hours: 9:00 PM – Late, every night.
Location: North Gate, near the Old City.

8. The Roof

Located atop the Akyra Manor Hotel, The Roof provides stunning panoramic views of the city, making it one of Chiang Mai's most sought-after rooftop venues. It's an upscale venue for those who want to party with a view.

What to Expect:

Chill house music during the early evening, building to more energetic beats as the night progresses.

A glamorous rooftop atmosphere, complete with cocktails and a stylish crowd.

A great spot for those who want to mix socializing with dancing and enjoying the views.

Best For: Those looking for a luxurious night out with a view of the city.

Opening Hours: 6:00 PM – Late, every night.

Location: Akyra Manor Hotel, Nimmanhaemin Road.

Tips for Nightlife in Chiang Mai

Dress Code: Many upscale clubs enforce a dress code, so it's a good idea to dress smart-casual. Avoid flip-flops and shorts, especially at higher-end venues.

Cover Charge: Some clubs may have an entry fee, especially on weekends or during special events.

Transportation: Taxis and tuk-tuks are available to take you back to your hotel after a night out. However, it's advisable to use apps like Grab or have the number of a local tuk-tuk driver on hand for late-night trips.

PRACTICAL INFORMATION

Safety and Health Tips

Personal Safety

Stay Alert in Crowded Areas: While Chiang Mai is generally safe, it's still important to be cautious in busy areas like markets, night bazaars, and public transport. Pickpocketing can occur in crowded places, so always keep an eye on your belongings.

Avoid Unofficial Taxis and Tuk-Tuks: Always use reputable transport options like Grab (ride-sharing app) or ask your hotel to help arrange a tuk-tuk or taxi. If you choose a tuk-tuk or taxi from the street, agree on the price before getting in, as some drivers may overcharge tourists.

Be Cautious with Alcohol: Drink responsibly and never leave your drink unattended. Stick to bars and clubs with good reputations, and avoid accepting drinks from strangers.

Avoid Walking Alone Late at Night: While Chiang Mai is generally safe, it's a good idea to avoid isolated areas at night, particularly if you're walking alone. Use taxis or ride-hailing apps for getting around after dark.

Respect Local Customs: Thai culture values politeness and respect, so avoid public displays of anger or frustration. Dress modestly, especially when visiting temples, and be respectful of local traditions.

Road Safety

Wear a Helmet When Riding a Scooter: If you rent a scooter or motorcycle, always wear a helmet, as this is required by law in Thailand. Driving can be chaotic, so ensure you're comfortable with the road conditions before taking one for a spin.

Be Careful on the Roads: Thailand has a high rate of traffic accidents. If you're not used to driving in busy areas or navigating narrow lanes, it's safer to rely on public transport or taxis.

Pedestrian Safety: Always use pedestrian crossings, as traffic in Chiang Mai can be unpredictable. Be cautious when crossing roads, especially in areas with heavy traffic.

Health Tips

Stay Hydrated: Chiang Mai can get very hot, especially from March to May. Carry a water bottle with you at all times and drink plenty of fluids to avoid dehydration. Be sure to also drink bottled water rather than tap water.

Sunscreen Protection: The sun in Chiang Mai can be intense. Use a broad-spectrum sunscreen with a high SPF to protect your skin from harmful UV rays. Reapply throughout the day, particularly if you're spending time outdoors.

Insect Protection: Mosquitoes can be a problem in Chiang Mai, especially during the rainy season. To avoid bites and potential diseases like dengue fever, use insect repellent, wear long-sleeved clothing, and sleep under a mosquito net if staying in areas with many mosquitoes.

Stay Cool: Avoid heat exhaustion by staying in the shade when possible and taking breaks if you're exploring on foot during the hottest parts of the day. Wear a hat or cap and loose, light clothing to keep cool.

Vaccinations: Ensure you are up to date with routine vaccinations before traveling to Thailand. Recommended vaccines for travelers to Chiang Mai may include Hepatitis A,

Hepatitis B, Typhoid, and Tetanus. Consult your healthcare provider before you travel.

Be Cautious with Street Food: While street food is an essential part of the Chiang Mai experience, it's important to ensure the food is cooked fresh and served hot. If you're not used to spicy foods, start slow to avoid stomach discomfort.

Emergency Contacts

Emergency Numbers: It's important to have the local emergency numbers handy:

Police: 191
Ambulance and Medical Assistance: 1669
Tourist Police: 1155
Fire Department: 199

Hospital Information: If you need medical assistance, Chiang Mai Ram Hospital and Santisuk Hospital are two well-known private hospitals in the city with English-speaking staff. The Chiang Mai Provincial Hospital is also available for more affordable treatment.

Travel Insurance: Ensure you have comprehensive travel insurance that covers medical emergencies, accidents, and theft. This is especially important for adventurous activities like trekking, zip-lining, or riding a scooter.

Food and Water Safety

Drink Bottled Water: Although Chiang Mai has a relatively good water treatment system, it's still safer to drink bottled water, particularly in rural areas or when traveling outside the city.
Street Food Safety: Street food in Chiang Mai is delicious, but be mindful of where you eat. Look for vendors with a high turnover of customers and freshly cooked food. If you're concerned about food hygiene, consider eating at well-established restaurants or food courts.
Avoid Ice in Drinks: Unless you're certain the ice has been made from purified water, avoid ice in your drinks. Stick to bottled drinks or beverages with no ice to avoid potential stomach issues.

Avoiding Scams

Tuk-Tuk and Taxi Scams: Always agree on a fare before getting in a tuk-tuk or taxi. Be wary of tuk-tuk drivers extending "tourist deals" that involve visits to various shops or gem stores, as these can often be scams.

Temple and Tour Scams: Some tuk-tuk drivers may provide tours to temples or attractions at discounted prices, but the driver might take you to a gem shop or other sales venues where they earn commissions. It's best to do your research and book tours through reputable companies or your hotel.

Currency Exchange: Only exchange money at licensed currency exchange booths or banks. Avoid exchanging money with individuals on the street, as you may be provide ed unfavorable rates or fake bills.

General Travel Tips

Language: While most people in Chiang Mai can communicate in English, especially in tourist areas, learning a few basic Thai phrases can help. Simple phrases like "hello" (Sawasdee), "thank you" (Khob Khun), and "how much?" (Tao rai?) can go a long way.

Respecting Sacred Sites: When visiting temples, make sure to dress modestly. Cover your shoulders and knees, remove shoes before entering temple buildings, and always act respectfully towards monks and religious objects.

Cash and Cards: While credit and debit cards are widely accepted in larger establishments, many small shops and markets only accept cash. ATMs are widely available, but it's best to carry some cash with you, especially in rural areas or when visiting markets.

Packing Essentials

1. Clothing Essentials

Light, Breathable Clothing: Chiang Mai has a tropical climate, so pack light, breathable clothes made from cotton or linen to stay cool. Think t-shirts, tank tops, shorts, skirts, and dresses. If you're traveling during the hot season (March-May), lightweight and loose-fitting clothes are key.
Modest Clothing for Temple Visits: When visiting temples, you'll need to dress modestly. Bring long pants or skirts and shirts that cover your shoulders. Avoid shorts, sleeveless tops, and revealing clothing in religious sites.
Comfortable Footwear: Bring comfortable walking shoes or sandals for city exploration. If you plan on trekking or hiking, sturdy shoes or hiking boots are a must. You may also want to

pack flip-flops or sandals for hotel showers and casual outings.

Light Jacket or Sweater: The weather can get cooler in the evenings, especially during the cool season (November to February), so a light jacket or sweater is advisable. If you plan on visiting the mountains, it can get chilly, so consider packing a warmer layer.

Swimwear: If you plan on swimming, pack swimwear. Many hotels and resorts in Chiang Mai have pools, and you may also want to visit hot springs.

2. Health and Hygiene

Sunscreen: The sun in Chiang Mai can be intense, so pack a high-SPF sunscreen to protect your skin from sunburn. Reapply regularly throughout the day, especially if you're spending time outdoors.

Insect Repellent: Chiang Mai, particularly during the rainy season (May–October), can have mosquitoes. Pack insect repellent with DEET or natural alternatives like citronella to prevent bites and protect yourself from diseases like dengue.

Hand Sanitizer and Wet Wipes: While public bathrooms are often available, having hand sanitizer and wet wipes can be handy when you're on the go, especially in more rural or rustic areas.

Medication and First Aid Kit: Bring any necessary prescription medications and basic over-the-counter remedies such as pain relievers, stomach medications, antihistamines, and any specific items you need. It's always helpful to have a basic first-aid kit with band-aids, antiseptic wipes, and other essentials.

Water Bottle: Staying hydrated is important, especially in the heat. Carry a reusable water bottle to refill throughout the day.

Vitamins and Supplements: If you take any daily vitamins or supplements, don't forget to pack them. You may also want to pack electrolyte tablets to help with hydration if you're spending long hours outside.

3. Travel Essentials

Passport and Copies: Ensure your passport is valid for at least six months beyond your planned departure date. It's also a good idea to make photocopies of your passport and keep them in a separate location, in case your original is lost or stolen.

Travel Insurance: Make sure you have travel insurance that covers health, accidents, and stolen or lost belongings. Carry a copy of your insurance details as well as any important contact numbers.

Currency and Cards: While ATMs are readily available in Chiang Mai, it's advisable to carry a small amount of Thai Baht (THB) in cash, especially when visiting markets or rural areas. Don't forget your credit or debit cards for payments at larger establishments.

Travel Adapter: Thailand uses Type A, B, and C power plugs, with a standard voltage of 220V. If your devices use a different plug type, bring a suitable adapter.

Mobile Phone and Charger: Don't forget your phone and charger. It's also useful to download essential apps like Grab for taxis, Maps.me for offline maps, and Google Translate to help with language.

4. Electronics and Gadgets

Camera: Chiang Mai provides many stunning sights, so bring a good camera to capture the beauty of temples, nature, and vibrant markets. If you don't have a dedicated camera, your smartphone will do.

Power Bank: Carry a portable charger to keep your devices charged throughout the day, especially if you plan on using your phone for navigation, photos, or translation.

Headphones: Useful for listening to music, podcasts, or using your phone during travel, whether you're on public transport or relaxing at a café.

E-reader or Book: If you enjoy reading, consider bringing an e-reader for easy access to books. Chiang Mai's laid-back atmosphere is perfect for reading in cafes or parks.

5. Miscellaneous Items

Backpack or Day Bag: A small day bag is ideal for daily sightseeing trips. It's helpful for carrying your camera, water bottle, sunscreen, and any other small essentials as you explore.

Plastic Bags: Pack a few foldable plastic bags for storing laundry or carrying items you pick up during the day, like food or souvenirs.

Tissues or Toilet Paper: Some public restrooms in Chiang Mai may not provide toilet paper, so it's a good idea to carry a small pack of tissues with you, especially when traveling outside of major tourist areas.

Ziplock Bags: Useful for storing snacks, toiletries, or small souvenirs without worrying about leaks or spills.

Snacks: If you're traveling long distances to visit nearby areas, having some snacks on hand can be a lifesaver. You can also try local snacks once you're in Chiang Mai.

6. Special Considerations for Adventure Travelers

Hiking Gear: If you're planning on trekking in Chiang Mai's national parks or mountains, pack sturdy hiking boots, a hat, and a rain jacket for unexpected downpours.

Camera Accessories: If you want to capture action shots or scenic landscapes, bring a tripod, extra memory cards, and extra batteries for your camera.

Waterproof Bag or Dry Sack: If you plan on doing activities like river cruising, zip-lining, or visiting waterfalls, pack a waterproof bag to protect your electronics and valuables from water damage.

Travel Pillow and Blanket: If you're taking long bus rides or going on overnight trips to nearby areas, a travel pillow and lightweight blanket can make your journey more comfortable.

7. Things to Leave at Home

Expensive Jewelry: It's best to leave valuable jewelry at home to avoid attracting unwanted attention or the risk of losing it.

Heavy Books: Instead of bringing bulky books, opt for an e-reader to save space in your luggage.

Over-the-Counter Medicines: You can easily purchase common medicines like painkillers, cold remedies, or antacids in Chiang Mai, so leave the heavy pharmaceutical items behind.

Emergency Contacts

1. Emergency Services

Police:
191
For general police emergencies, including theft or accidents.

Ambulance and Medical Assistance:
1669
For medical emergencies, ambulance services, or medical assistance.

Fire Department:

199

In case of fire or immediate fire-related emergency.

2. Tourist Police

Tourist Police:

1155

A dedicated police service that speaks English and is designed to assist tourists in case of emergencies or problems. They can help with lost passports, scams, or general security concerns.

3. Hospitals and Medical Assistance

Chiang Mai Ram Hospital (Private Hospital):

+66 53 999 200

One of the most well-known private hospitals in Chiang Mai with international standards.

Santisuk Hospital (Private Hospital):

+66 53 249 199

Another private hospital in Chiang Mai, extending English-speaking staff and modern medical services.

Chiang Mai Provincial Hospital (Public Hospital):
+66 53 891 254
For affordable medical care, this public hospital provides both general and emergency services.

International Medical Clinic (IMC):
+66 53 904 788
Located in the Nimmanhaemin area, IMC is popular among expats and tourists for medical consultations and general health services.

4. Embassies and Consulates

U.S. Consular Agency in Chiang Mai:
+66 53 107 700
For U.S. citizens needing assistance with consular services, emergencies, or passport issues.

British Embassy in Bangkok (with consular services in Chiang Mai):
+66 2 305 8333
The British embassy provides consular services, including lost or stolen passports and legal assistance.

Australian Consulate-General in Chiang Mai:
+66 53 894 400
For Australians in need of consular support, legal advice, or assistance with emergencies.

Canadian Consulate in Chiang Mai:
+66 53 257 880
For Canadians needing consular services, including emergency help, passport replacement, and legal issues.

5. General Travel Assistance

Tourism Authority of Thailand (TAT) Chiang Mai Office:
+66 53 248 604
If you need information or assistance with travel plans, activities, or local attractions.

Thai Red Cross Society (For medical emergencies and blood donations):
+66 2 256 4101
The Thai Red Cross provides support for medical emergencies and can help in disaster relief situations.

6. Taxi and Transportation Services

Chiang Mai Grab (Ride-Hailing App):
Download the Grab app
For safe and reliable ride-hailing services in Chiang Mai. You can call a Grab taxi or private car, which is a safer option than hailing one from the street.

Chiang Mai Airport Information:
+66 53 285 000
For assistance related to flights, lost luggage, or airport services.

7. Additional Numbers

Lost Property (Chiang Mai) - Police Station:
+66 53 276 295
For recovering lost items or filing reports about lost property.

Chiang Mai Post Office:
+66 53 231 228
For general inquiries or services related to mail or shipping.

Important General Safety Tips

Always have your passport, hotel contact details, and travel insurance information handy in case of emergencies.
Keep a copy of emergency contacts in both digital and printed formats for easy access.
If you're not sure about which emergency service to call, Tourist Police (1155) can direct you to the appropriate assistance in English.

Internet and Communication

Mobile Networks and SIM Cards

Thailand has several mobile carriers with good coverage throughout Chiang Mai, including in rural areas. Most tourists opt to buy a local SIM card upon arrival for easy access to mobile data and local calls.

Mobile Network Providers:

AIS (Advanced Info Service):
One of the largest networks in Thailand, known for its reliable coverage and fast data speed. They provide prepaid SIM cards with data

packages, which are perfect for short-term travelers.

TrueMove H:
Another major network, extending similar prepaid SIM cards with good coverage and affordable data plans. They also have deals with various data options tailored for tourists.

DTAC (Total Access Communication):
Popular for its competitive pricing and good network coverage, DTAC provides various SIM card packages and data deals for tourists.

Where to Buy SIM Cards:

Chiang Mai International Airport:
SIM cards can be easily purchased from kiosks at the airport upon arrival. The staff usually speaks English, and they can assist you in choosing the best package.

7-Eleven Convenience Stores:
These are abundant across Chiang Mai and provide SIM cards for sale. You can buy a SIM card and top it up with data and credit easily.

Mobile Carrier Shops:
You can also visit official shops for the mobile carriers (AIS, TrueMove, or DTAC) in shopping malls like Central Festival Chiang Mai or in the city center.

Data Plans and Price Range:

SIM Cards: Typically cost around 100–200 THB ($3–6 USD) for a basic package, which includes some credit and a few gigabytes of data.

Data Packages: Prices vary depending on the amount of data you need. 1GB–3GB of data usually costs around 100–300 THB ($3–9 USD), and some plans include unlimited calls within Thailand.

Important Tips:

Make sure your phone is unlocked before arriving to use a local SIM card.

Be sure to bring a copy of your passport for registration when purchasing a SIM card, as this is required for all mobile contracts in Thailand.

Wi-Fi Availability

Wi-Fi is widely available in Chiang Mai, and many cafes, restaurants, hotels, and public places provide free internet access.

Common Wi-Fi Locations:

Hotels and Hostels:
Most hotels and guesthouses in Chiang Mai provide free Wi-Fi to guests. However, the quality and speed can vary, especially in more budget-friendly accommodations.

Cafes and Restaurants:
Many cafes and eateries cater to digital nomads and tourists by extending free Wi-Fi. Popular cafes like Ristr8to, The Blue Diamond Café, and The Barn: Eatery Design have excellent Wi-Fi connections.

Shopping Malls:
Major malls like Central Festival Chiang Mai and MAYA Lifestyle Shopping Center provide free Wi-Fi, making it easy to stay connected while you shop.

Co-working Spaces:
For those who need reliable Wi-Fi for work,
Chiang Mai has a growing number of
co-working spaces such as PunSpace, Yellow
Coworking, and WeWork. These spaces usually
provide fast internet and a quiet, productive
environment.

Internet Speed and Costs:

Internet Speed: In general, the internet speed
in Chiang Mai is fast in urban areas, with an
average speed of 20–30 Mbps. Speeds can be
slower in rural or more remote areas.

Internet Costs:
If you're using mobile data, most data plans
allow you to use the internet for 3G or 4G
speeds. Some cafes and co-working spaces may
charge a small fee for Wi-Fi if you don't make a
purchase.

Calling and Messaging

Making Local Calls:

To make local calls within Thailand, simply use
your SIM card. For international calls, you can

use VoIP services or buy calling cards for cheaper rates.

Local Calls: Typically, 5–10 THB ($0.15–0.30 USD) per minute for local calls.

International Calls: For international calling, you can either use your mobile phone with international dialing codes or purchase a calling card for cheaper rates. Alternatively, VoIP services like Skype or WhatsApp are widely used for international communication over Wi-Fi.

Messaging Apps:

LINE:
One of the most popular messaging apps in Thailand. It's used widely for both personal and business communications. You can send text messages, voice messages, and make calls via Wi-Fi or mobile data.

WhatsApp:
WhatsApp is also commonly used in Chiang Mai, especially for international communication, as it uses your phone's internet connection rather than traditional SMS.

Facebook Messenger:
Another popular app for messaging. Many businesses and tourists also use Facebook Messenger for communication in Chiang Mai.

Public Phones

Public phones are becoming rare in Chiang Mai, and it's more common to use mobile phones or apps for communication. However, if you need to use a payphone:

Payphones are available at some public places, but you'll need to use a phone card. These can be purchased at kiosks or convenience stores like 7-Eleven.

Internet Cafes

While most people prefer to use their mobile devices or laptops with Wi-Fi, some traditional internet cafes can still be found in Chiang Mai for those who need access to a computer or internet connection.

Cost: Generally, 20–40 THB ($0.60–1.20 USD) per hour for computer use in internet cafes.

Staying Secure Online

While in Chiang Mai, it's important to protect your personal information when using public Wi-Fi. Here are some tips to stay safe online: Use a VPN: Consider using a Virtual Private Network (VPN) when connected to public Wi-Fi to protect your personal data and ensure a secure internet connection.
Avoid Sensitive Transactions on Public Wi-Fi: Refrain from making financial transactions or accessing sensitive information while on public Wi-Fi networks unless you are using a VPN.

Visa and Entry Requirements for Chiang Mai (Thailand)

1. Visa Exemption (Tourist Visa-Free Entry)

Many nationalities can enter Thailand for short visits (usually up to 30 days) without the need for a visa. This is known as the Visa Exemption.

Countries Eligible for Visa Exemption:
Citizens of the European Union (e.g., United Kingdom, France, Germany, etc.)

United States
Canada
Australia
New Zealand
Japan
South Korea
Singapore
Malaysia
Hong Kong
South Africa

These travelers can stay for up to 30 days without a visa when entering Thailand by air, and up to 15 days if entering by land from a neighboring country. Make sure your passport is valid for at least six months beyond your intended stay.

2. Tourist Visa (for longer stays or specific nationalities)

If you're planning to stay in Thailand for more than 30 days or if you're from a country that doesn't qualify for the visa exemption, you'll need to apply for a Tourist Visa.

Tourist Visa Types:

Single Entry Tourist Visa:
Allows you to stay in Thailand for 60 days from the date of entry. You can apply for an extension of up to 30 days at the Immigration Office.

Multiple Entry Tourist Visa (METV):
Allows you to stay in Thailand for 60 days per entry, and you can re-enter the country up to multiple times within a six-month period.

How to Apply for a Tourist Visa:

You can apply for a Tourist Visa at the Thai embassy or consulate in your home country or a nearby country.

Documents typically required include:
Valid passport (with at least six months' validity)
Completed visa application form
Passport-sized photos
Proof of onward travel (such as a flight ticket)
Proof of financial stability (bank statements)
Visa fee (typically around 1,000–1,500 THB)

3. Visa on Arrival (VOA)

Citizens of certain countries are eligible for a Visa on Arrival (VOA) when entering Thailand. This visa allows you to stay for up to 15 days.

Countries Eligible for VOA:
India
China
Pakistan
Bangladesh
Sri Lanka
Maldives
Nepal
Bhutan
Taiwan (certain conditions apply)

Requirements for Visa on Arrival:

Valid passport (at least six months validity)
Completed Visa on Arrival form
Passport-sized photos
10,000 THB per person (or equivalent in foreign currency)
Return flight ticket or onward travel ticket proving departure from Thailand within 15 days

Visa Fee: Usually around 2,000 THB (subject to change).

4. Thailand Elite Visa (Long-Term Visa)

For those who wish to stay in Thailand for an extended period, the Thailand Elite Visa provides long-term stays with various benefits, including airport fast-track services, concierge services, and more.

Thailand Elite Visa Options:

Elite Easy Access (5 years): Costs around 500,000 THB.
Elite Family Excursion (5 years): Costs around 800,000 THB for up to 2 persons.
Elite Ultimate Privilege (20 years): Costs around 1,000,000 THB.

The Thailand Elite Visa is an option for those who want a long-term stay without the need to leave and re-enter the country.

Extensions of Stay

If you're already in Thailand and wish to extend your stay, you can apply for an extension of stay at a local Immigration Office.
Tourist visa extensions are typically granted for an additional 30 days.
Visa on Arrival (VOA) extensions are generally not available.

Costs for an extension vary, but you can expect to pay around 1,900 THB for a 30-day extension.

Border Runs

If you entered Thailand under the visa exemption and want to stay longer, you can do a border run by leaving the country and returning. This can be done by traveling to a nearby country (such as Laos, Myanmar, or Cambodia), and then re-entering Thailand to reset the 30-day period.

Important Entry Requirements

Passport Validity: Ensure that your passport is valid for at least six months beyond your intended stay.

Proof of Funds: Immigration officers may ask for proof of sufficient funds (typically 10,000 THB per person or 20,000 THB per family) to ensure you can support yourself during your stay in Thailand.

Return or Onward Ticket: When entering Thailand, you may be required to show proof of your return or onward travel ticket, proving you will leave Thailand within your permitted stay.

Special Considerations During COVID-19 (if applicable)

As of the current regulations, Thailand may have specific health and safety measures in place, such as:

COVID-19 testing requirements before travel (depending on the situation).

Proof of vaccinations for some travelers (varies depending on nationality).

Travel insurance that covers COVID-19 medical expenses (often required for long-term or visa applications).

Check the Thai Ministry of Foreign Affairs or your local Thai embassy website for the latest updates before traveling.

Entry via Land Border

If you're traveling to Chiang Mai by land from a neighboring country like Laos or Myanmar, you may be subject to different entry requirements, such as:

15-day entry limit for land border arrivals (unless eligible for the 30-day visa exemption by air).
Visa requirements if you're from a country not eligible for the visa exemption.

Language

Thai Language

Overview
Thai (or Central Thai) is the official language of Thailand. It is a tonal language, which means that the tone or pitch used when pronouncing a word can change its meaning. Thai uses the Thai script, which may look intimidating to beginners, but learning a few key words and phrases can help enhance your experience.

Common Phrases to Know in Thai:

Hello: สวัสดี (Sawasdee)
How are you?: สบายดีไหม (Sabaidee Mai?)
Thank you: ขอบคุณ (Khob Khun)
Yes: ใช่ (Chai)
No: ไม่ (Mai)
Excuse me / Sorry: ขอโทษ (Khor Thot)
Goodbye: ลาก่อน (La Korn)

Tonal Language

Thai has five tones (high, mid, low, rising, and falling), and the meaning of a word can change based on the tone used. For example:

Mái (ไม้) means "wood" when pronounced with a high tone but "new" (ใหม่) when pronounced with a rising tone.

While understanding the tonal system is essential for fluency, you'll likely be able to get by with simple phrases, especially if you focus on speaking clearly and slowly.

Northern Thai (Lanna)

Chiang Mai is located in the northern part of Thailand, and the local population speaks Northern Thai (also called Lanna). It's a regional dialect, and while it's related to standard Thai, it has unique vocabulary, pronunciation, and some differences in grammar.

Key Points About Lanna:

Northern Thai vs. Thai: People in Chiang Mai may use Northern Thai in informal settings, especially with friends, family, or in rural areas. However, Thai remains the language of business, education, and government.
Lanna Influence: Many signs and phrases in Chiang Mai, especially in tourist areas, may

include Lanna expressions. Some older generations may still speak Lanna exclusively. Lanna Writing: The Lanna script is distinct from the standard Thai script, though it is not widely used in daily life anymore. It is primarily seen in cultural and religious contexts.

Common Phrases in Northern Thai (Lanna):

Hello: สวัสดี (Sawasdee) [Same as in Thai]
How are you?: สบายดีหรือเปล่า (Sabaidee Reu Blah?)
Thank you: ขอบใจ (Khob Jai) [Alternative to "Khob Khun" in standard Thai]

English in Chiang Mai

English Usage

Tourist Areas: In Chiang Mai's most popular tourist areas (such as the Old City, Nimmanhaemin, and major attractions), you'll find that many people can communicate in English to some degree. This includes hotel staff, tour operators, and restaurant employees. Non-Tourist Areas: Outside of tourist hubs, English proficiency may be lower. However, many younger Thais (especially in Chiang Mai) understand basic English due to their education.

Practical Tips for English Speakers:

Learn Basic Thai Phrases: Even though you may not be fluent, learning a few key Thai words can go a long way in creating goodwill and improving communication.
Use Gestures: If you're struggling with a language barrier, don't hesitate to use hand gestures or show pictures on your phone to help convey your message.
Google Translate: The Google Translate app is a useful tool when you need help translating written or spoken text between Thai and English.

Other Languages

Chiang Mai's growing expat community has brought in a variety of languages, especially in certain neighborhoods like Nimmanhaemin. Additionally, the city has a mix of ethnic minorities, and you may encounter other languages, including:

Chinese: Due to Chiang Mai's historical and commercial connections with China, there's a noticeable presence of Chinese speakers, especially in certain areas and businesses.

Karen and Other Hill Tribe Languages: Chiang Mai is close to several hill tribe regions, and languages such as Karen, Hmong, and Lahu are spoken in more rural areas.

Writing System

While the Thai script is the official writing system in Thailand, you may encounter both Thai script and Romanization (English characters) in signage and menus in tourist areas. For example, restaurant menus or signs at popular attractions may include both the Thai and English names, making it easier for tourists to navigate.

Thai Script and Romanization:

Thai Script: It's a unique alphabet with 44 consonants and 15 vowel symbols, which can make it challenging to read for beginners.

Romanization: Some Thai words may be written in the Latin alphabet, but the pronunciation can be different from English. For instance, the Thai word for "thank you" (ขอบคุณ) is written as khop khun in Romanized form.

Learning Thai in Chiang Mai

Chiang Mai is an excellent place to learn Thai due to its welcoming atmosphere, abundant language schools, and cultural richness. If you're planning a longer stay or want to improve your language skills, there are many language schools extending Thai language courses for foreigners.

Popular Language Schools in Chiang Mai:

AUA Language Center Chiang Mai: A well-known school extending structured Thai language programs for beginners to advanced learners.
Chiang Mai University's Thai Language Program: provides a more formal course, with options for learning Thai for work, study, or cultural immersion.
Thai with Mod: A more informal and flexible option, perfect for travelers looking to learn key phrases or practice Thai conversation.

Communication Etiquette in Chiang Mai

Understanding a few cultural nuances around communication can enhance your experience in Chiang Mai:

Polite Language: Thai people tend to speak very politely, often using the word "krub" (for males) or "ka" (for females) at the end of sentences to show respect.
Respect for Elders: Always show respect when addressing elders, and avoid raising your voice or appearing confrontational.
Smiling: The Thai smile is an important part of communication and is used in many social situations to convey friendliness, calmness, or sometimes to defuse tension.

SUGGESTED ITINERARIES

5-Day Itinerary

Day 1: Arrival and Exploring the Old City

Morning:

Arrive in Chiang Mai and check into your hotel. Begin your exploration with a stroll around Chiang Mai Old City. This area is rich in history, with its ancient walls, temples, and relaxed atmosphere.
Wat Phra Singh: Famous for its impressive Lanna architecture and peaceful atmosphere.
Wat Chedi Luang: An ancient temple with a beautiful pagoda and a rich history, including housing the Emerald Buddha for a period.

Lunch:

Enjoy a meal at one of the many cafes or street food stalls in the Old City. Try Khao Soi (a traditional northern Thai noodle dish).

Afternoon:

Explore the Old City Walls and Gates: Visit the Tha Phae Gate, one of the main entry points to the Old City.
Take a walking tour of the nearby art galleries and local shops.

Evening:

Head to the Sunday Walking Street Market (if it's Sunday) for shopping and street food. The market provides a wide range of handicrafts, clothing, and delicious local delicacies.
Alternatively, have a relaxed dinner at a traditional Thai restaurant, such as Huen Phen or Kantoke Dining for a cultural meal experience.

Day 2: Temples and Cultural Immersion

Morning:

Doi Suthep Temple: Visit one of Chiang Mai's most famous temples, Wat Phra That Doi Suthep. The view of Chiang Mai from the temple is spectacular. Be prepared for a steep climb or take a cable car up.

Explore Doi Suthep National Park: Take some time to walk around the park and enjoy the fresh air and nature.

Lunch:

Have lunch at a local restaurant near the base of Doi Suthep, or in the Nimmanhaemin area.

Afternoon:

Wat Umong: Visit this tranquil, ancient temple set in the forest. Known for its underground tunnels, it provides a peaceful escape from the hustle and bustle of the city.
Chiang Mai University Art Center: Head over to this gallery for a dose of local contemporary art.

Evening:

Enjoy dinner in Nimmanhaemin — a trendy neighborhood with great restaurants and cafes.
Relax with a drink at one of the city's famous rooftop bars, such as the Sala Lanna Rooftop or The Roof at the Akyra Manor.

Day 3: Nature, Adventure, and Hill Tribes

Morning:

Elephant Sanctuary: Spend the morning at an ethical elephant sanctuary, like the Elephant Nature Park. Learn about elephant conservation, feed the elephants, and even take a walk with them through the lush jungle.

Lunch:

Enjoy a traditional Thai lunch at the sanctuary or nearby restaurant.

Afternoon:

After visiting the sanctuary, head out on a trekking tour in the mountains surrounding Chiang Mai. Many tour operators provide half-day treks to explore the jungle, meet local hill tribes, and hike to scenic spots like waterfalls.

Evening:

Return to Chiang Mai and relax after your adventure.

Dinner at The Riverside Bar & Restaurant by the Ping River provides a beautiful view and a great mix of Thai and international dishes.

Day 4: Day Trip to Chiang Rai and the White Temple

Morning:

Early morning departure to Chiang Rai: The drive to Chiang Rai takes about 3 hours. Stop along the way to admire the scenic views and visit local villages.
Wat Rong Khun (White Temple): This is the main highlight of the trip. The temple is an incredibly intricate and unique modern Buddhist structure. It's one of the most iconic temples in Thailand.

Lunch:

Enjoy lunch at a local restaurant in Chiang Rai, trying dishes such as Khao Soi (noodle soup) or Nam Ngiao (a northern Thai noodle dish).

Afternoon:

Blue Temple (Wat Rong Suea Ten): Another stunning modern temple known for its deep blue tones and beautiful murals.
Baan Dam (Black House): Visit the Black House for a glimpse of a collection of quirky, dark art pieces and traditional northern Thai architecture.

Evening:

Drive back to Chiang Mai and relax after the day's adventure. Consider a quiet dinner at one of the local eateries near your hotel.

Day 5: Adventure and Relaxation

Morning:

Zip lining and Jungle Adventure: Book a zip-line tour through the lush rainforest surrounding Chiang Mai. This is an adrenaline-pumping way to see the forest from a new perspective.

Lunch:

After your thrilling experience, enjoy a well-earned lunch in Hang Dong or near the Mae Wang area.

Afternoon:

Hot Springs in Chiang Dao: Head to Chiang Dao for a relaxing soak in natural hot springs surrounded by mountains. You can also explore the nearby Chiang Dao Cave for a short trek and spiritual experience.

Evening:

For your last night in Chiang Mai, explore the Night Bazaar for some shopping, last-minute souvenirs, and street food.
Enjoy a farewell dinner at The Good View or Riverside Bar & Restaurant, extending great food and riverside views.

Additional Tips:

Transport: Rent a scooter or take taxis for easy access to remote locations.

Weather: Dress comfortably, especially for temple visits and trekking tours. Don't forget sunscreen, a hat, and comfortable shoes.

Booking Tours: Some of these activities, such as elephant sanctuaries and trekking tours, require advanced bookings.

7-Day Itinerary

Day 1: Arrival and Exploring the Old City

Morning:

Arrive in Chiang Mai and check into your hotel. Begin your exploration by walking around the Old City. Visit the iconic Tha Phae Gate and take in the sights of the ancient city walls.

Lunch:

Enjoy a light lunch at a local café in the Old City, such as The Salad Concept or a nearby street food stall.

Afternoon:

Wat Phra Singh: Visit this temple with its classic Lanna architecture.
Wat Chedi Luang: Explore this ancient and historically significant temple.
Walk around the Old City Walls and discover the local shops and art galleries.

Evening:

Explore the Sunday Walking Street Market (if it's Sunday) or Saturday Night Market for handicrafts, street food, and local products.
Enjoy dinner at a local restaurant, such as Huen Phen, serving authentic northern Thai cuisine.

Day 2: Temples, Doi Suthep, and Scenic Views

Morning:

Doi Suthep Temple: Visit one of the most famous temples in Chiang Mai, Wat Phra That Doi Suthep. The temple is located on a mountain with spectacular views of Chiang Mai. You can either take the stairs or the cable car to the top.

Lunch:

Have lunch at a local restaurant in the Doi Suthep area or head back to the city for a meal.

Afternoon:

Doi Suthep National Park: After visiting the temple, take some time to explore the lush surroundings of the national park, which provides nature trails and cool mountain air.
Visit Wat Umong, an ancient temple with underground tunnels set in a forest.

Evening:

Return to Chiang Mai and relax.
Head to Nimmanhaemin for a trendy dinner spot and enjoy the evening ambiance at one of its rooftop bars.

Day 3: Nature and Adventure

Morning:

Elephant Sanctuary: Spend the day at an ethical elephant sanctuary like Elephant Nature Park or Elephant Jungle Sanctuary. Learn about the conservation efforts, feed and bathe the elephants, and enjoy a nature-filled experience.

Lunch:

Enjoy a traditional Thai lunch at the sanctuary or nearby restaurant.

Afternoon:

After the elephant sanctuary visit, take a trek through the nearby jungles or enjoy a peaceful time by the river.

Evening:

Head back to Chiang Mai and relax after a day of adventure.
Dinner at a riverside restaurant such as The Riverside Bar & Restaurant, extending scenic views and delicious food.

Day 4: Day Trip to Chiang Rai and the White Temple

Morning:

Early morning departure to Chiang Rai (about 3 hours). Stop at Singha Park for scenic views and a relaxing coffee break.

Lunch:

Enjoy lunch at a local restaurant in Chiang Rai.

Afternoon:

Wat Rong Khun (White Temple): Explore the stunning White Temple, one of the most unique temples in Thailand, designed by artist Chalermchai Kositpipat.
Blue Temple (Wat Rong Suea Ten): Visit this striking blue temple for its beautiful murals and vibrant colors.
Baan Dam (Black House): Explore this eclectic art museum, known for its dark, unconventional style.

Evening:

Drive back to Chiang Mai.
Enjoy a quiet evening with dinner at a local eatery or at your hotel.

Day 5: Hill Tribe Villages and Nature Exploration

Morning:

Day Trip to Pai: Drive or take a minibus to Pai, a charming town in the mountains about 3 hours north of Chiang Mai. On the way, enjoy the scenic landscapes of the Pai Canyon and Pai Hot Springs.

Lunch:

Have lunch at a local Pai café or restaurant, trying dishes such as Khao Soi or Pad Thai.

Afternoon:

Hill Tribe Village Visit: Explore Pai's nearby hill tribe villages to learn about the unique cultures and traditions of ethnic groups such as the Karen, Lahu, and Hmong people.

Alternatively, you can explore Pai's Walking Street Market for local goods and artisan products.

Evening:

Return to Chiang Mai in the evening.
Relax and enjoy a low-key dinner in one of Chiang Mai's popular restaurants.

Day 6: Adventure Activities and Local Culture

Morning:

Ziplining: Spend the morning ziplining through the jungle at Flight of the Gibbon or another nearby zip-lining adventure company. Enjoy the adrenaline rush as you soar over the forest canopy.

Lunch:

Head to a nearby restaurant for lunch, and try local favorites like Sausage Sai Oua or Nam Prik Ong (a northern chili dip).

Afternoon:

After the ziplining, visit the Chiang Mai Zoo and Aquarium for a more relaxed activity, or check out the Chiang Mai Arts and Cultural Center for insights into the city's history and traditions.

Evening:

Enjoy a peaceful evening by the Mae Ping River.
For dinner, consider The Good View or another restaurant with a riverside view, extending delicious food and a relaxing atmosphere.

Day 7: Wellness and Relaxation

Morning:

Traditional Thai Massage: Start your last day with a traditional Thai massage at one of Chiang Mai's renowned spas. Consider visiting Fah Lanna Spa or Oasis Spa for a luxury experience.

Lunch:

Have a light lunch at a wellness café, such as The Green Pea or Melt In Your Mouth.

Afternoon:

Take a Mae Ping River Cruise to enjoy a scenic boat ride along the river, or visit Bua Thong Waterfalls (Sticky Waterfalls) where you can climb the limestone falls with ease due to their unique texture.
Explore some of Chiang Mai's local handicraft villages like Bo Sang for a traditional umbrella-making demonstration or San Kamphaeng for silverware and textiles.

Evening:

Farewell Dinner: End your trip with a memorable dinner at Kantoke Dinner, where you can enjoy traditional northern Thai food served in the traditional way with live cultural performances.

Additional Tips:

Transport: Rent a scooter or use taxis and Songthaews for easy access to locations outside of the city.

Weather: Dress in layers if visiting the mountains (Doi Suthep, Doi Inthanon) as it can be cooler than the city.

Local Etiquette: Be respectful in temples—dress modestly and remove your shoes before entering temple buildings.

CONCLUSION

Useful Phrases

Basic Greetings:

Hello / Hi – สวัสดี (sawasdee)
Goodbye – ลาก่อน (laa-gon)
Good Morning – สวัสดีตอนเช้า (sawasdee ton chao)
Good Evening – สวัสดีตอนเย็น (sawasdee ton yen)
How are you? – สบายดีไหม (sabai dee mai?)
I'm fine, thank you. – สบายดี ขอบคุณ (sabai dee, khop khun)
Thank you – ขอบคุณ (khop khun)
Sorry / Excuse me – ขอโทษ (khor thot)
Please – กรุณา (ka-ru-na)

At the Market or Shopping:

How much is this? – อันนี้ราคาเท่าไหร่ (an nee raa-khaa thao-rai?)
I want this. – เอานี่ (ao nee)
Can you give me a discount? – ลดราคาได้ไหม (lot raa-khaa dai mai?)

Too expensive – แพงเกินไป (phaeng gern pai)
Cheap – ถูก (thook)
I don't understand. – ฉันไม่เข้าใจ (chan mai khao jai)
Do you have...? – คุณมี...ไหม (khun mee... mai?)

Food and Drink:

What is this? – นี่คืออะไร (nee keu arai?)
I would like... – ฉันต้องการ... (chan tong-kaan...)
Spicy – เผ็ด (phet)
Not spicy – ไม่เผ็ด (mai phet)
Water – น้ำ (nam)
No sugar – ไม่มีน้ำตาล (mai mee nam-tan)
Vegetarian – มังสวิรัติ (mang-sa wi-rat)

Transportation and Directions:

Where is the taxi stand? – ที่จอดแท็กซี่อยู่ที่ไหน (thee jot taxi yoo thee nai?)
How do I get to...? – ไป...ยังไง (bpai... yang ngai?)
Left – ซ้าย (saai)
Right – ขวา (khwaa)
Straight – ตรงไป (trong bpai)
Near – ใกล้ (glai)
Far – ไกล (glai)
Stop here – หยุดที่นี่ (yut thee nee)

At the Temple:

Temple – วัด (wat)
Where is the bathroom? – ห้องน้ำอยู่ที่ไหน (hong nam yoo thee nai?)
I would like to pray. – ฉันต้องการสวดมนต์ (chan tong-kaan suat-mon)
Respectfully bow – กราบ (krab)

Emergency:

Help! – ช่วยด้วย (chuay duay)
Call the police! – เรียกตำรวจ! (riak tam-ruat)
I'm lost. – ฉันหลงทาง (chan long thang)
I'm sick. – ฉันป่วย (chan bpuay)
Hospital – โรงพยาบาล (rong pha-ya-baan)

General:

Yes – ใช่ (chai)
No – ไม่ (mai)
What's your name? – คุณชื่ออะไร (khun chue arai?)
My name is... – ฉันชื่อ... (chan chue...)
Nice to meet you. – ยินดีที่ได้รู้จัก (yin-dee tee dai roo-jak)

Useful Apps and Websites

Navigation and Transportation:

1. Grab (App)

Purpose: Ride-hailing app for taxis, motorbikes, and food delivery. It's widely used in Chiang Mai for getting around the city.
Download: iOS | Android

2. Google Maps (App & Website)

Purpose: Essential for navigating the city, finding restaurants, temples, and local businesses. It provides walking, biking, and driving directions.
Website: Google Maps

3. Songthaew (App)

Purpose: A local app that helps you track and hail Songthaews (shared red taxis) in Chiang Mai.
Download: iOS | Android

4. Tuk Tuk Chiang Mai (App)

Purpose: provides tuk-tuk services within Chiang Mai, making it easy to get around in the famous three-wheeled vehicles.
Download: iOS | Android

Language Translation:

5. Google Translate (App & Website)

Purpose: Helps with language translation between Thai and your native language. Useful when you're not familiar with Thai.
Download: iOS | Android
Website: Google Translate

6. SayHi Translate (App)

Purpose: A real-time translation app that can help you communicate directly with locals.
Download: iOS | Android

Travel Planning and Local Experiences:

7. TripAdvisor (App & Website)

Purpose: provides reviews, ratings, and recommendations for hotels, restaurants, tours, and activities in Chiang Mai. Great for researching where to eat and things to do.
Download: iOS | Android
Website: TripAdvisor

8. Klook (App & Website)

Purpose: Book local tours, activities, and experiences in Chiang Mai at discounted prices. Great for organizing day trips, tickets for temples, and excursions.
Download: iOS | Android
Website: Klook

9. TAT (Tourism Authority of Thailand) Official Website

Purpose: The official website provides a wealth of information about Chiang Mai, including things to do, festivals, and travel tips.
Website: Tourism Authority of Thailand

Food and Dining:

10. HappyCow (App & Website)

Purpose: Find vegan, vegetarian, and plant-based dining options around Chiang Mai.
Download: iOS | Android
Website: HappyCow

11. Eatigo (App)

Purpose: A dining app that provides restaurant deals, discounts, and reservations in Chiang Mai.
Download: iOS | Android

Shopping and Local Goods:

12. Line (App)

Purpose: A popular messaging app in Thailand used to communicate with local businesses, join group chats for events, and book services like taxis and delivery.
Download: iOS | Android

13. Shopee (App)

Purpose: A popular e-commerce app where you can shop for local products, clothing, and souvenirs.
Download: iOS | Android

Cultural and Activities Apps:

14. ThaiFind (App)

Purpose: Discover Chiang Mai's unique cultural activities, workshops, and tours. Great for finding things like cooking classes, art workshops, and local cultural experiences.
Download: iOS | Android

15. Couchsurfing (App & Website)

Purpose: Find a local host to stay with, or simply meet up with fellow travelers for social activities.
Download: iOS | Android
Website: Couchsurfing

Weather and Planning:

16. Weather Thailand (App)

Purpose: provides real-time weather updates, including forecasts specific to Chiang Mai. Great for planning your outdoor activities.
Download: iOS | Android

17. AccuWeather (App & Website)

Purpose: Another reliable weather app, providing forecasts, radar, and live updates.
Download: iOS | Android
Website: AccuWeather

Made in the USA
Las Vegas, NV
25 November 2024

12609433R00199